COLDPLAY
A RUSH OF BLOOD TO THE HEAD

GUITAR
TAB
EDITION

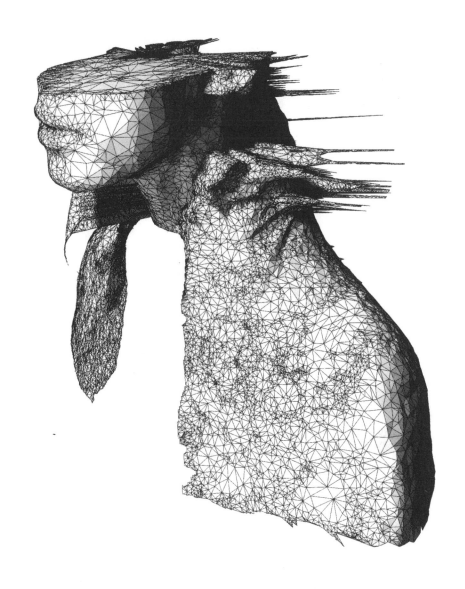

Exclusive distributors:

Music Sales Limited
8/9 Frith Street, London W1D 3JB,
England.

Music Sales Pty Limited
120 Rothschild Avenue, Rosebery, NSW 2018,
Australia.

Order No. AM975128
ISBN 0-7119-9605-9
This book © Copyright 2002 by Wise Publications.

Music arrangements by Arthur Dick.
Music processed by Paul Ewers Music Design.
Cover artwork courtesy of Blue Source.

Printed in the United Kingdom by
Caligraving Limited, Thetford, Norfolk.

www.musicsales.com

COLDPLAY
A RUSH OF BLOOD TO THE HEAD

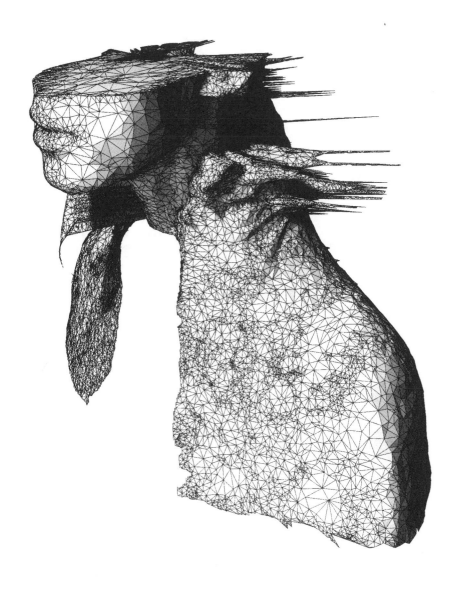

DISTRIBUTED BY

HAL•LEONARD®
CORPORATION
WINONA, MN 55987   MILWAUKEE, WI 53213

Wise Publications
London / New York / Paris / Sydney / Copenhagen / Berlin / Madrid / Tokyo

Guitar Tablature Explained

Guitar music can be notated three different ways: on a musical stave, in tablature, and in rhythm slashes.

RHYTHM SLASHES are written above the stave. Strum chords in the rhythm indicated. Round noteheads indicate single notes.

THE MUSICAL STAVE shows pitches and rhythms and is divided by lines into bars. Pitches are named after the first seven letters of the alphabet.

TABLATURE graphically represents the guitar fingerboard. Each horizontal line represents a string, and each number represents a fret.

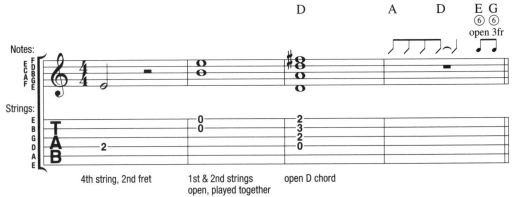

4th string, 2nd fret

1st & 2nd strings open, played together

open D chord

Definitions for Special Guitar Notation

SEMI-TONE BEND: Strike the note and bend up a semi-tone (1/2 step).

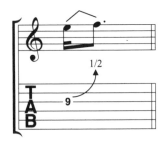

WHOLE-TONE BEND: Strike the note and bend up a whole-tone (whole step).

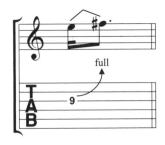

GRACE NOTE BEND: Strike the note and bend as indicated. Play the first note as quickly as possible.

QUARTER-TONE BEND: Strike the note and bend up a 1/4 step.

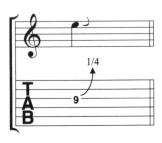

BEND & RELEASE: Strike the note and bend up as indicated, then release back to the original note.

COMPOUND BEND & RELEASE: Strike the note and bend up and down in the rhythm indicated.

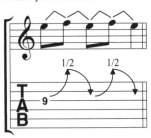

PRE-BEND: Bend the note as indicated, then strike it.

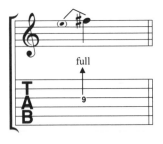

PRE-BEND & RELEASE: Bend the note as indicated. Strike it and release the note back to the original pitch.

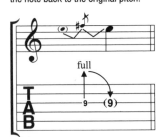

UNISON BEND: Strike the two notes simultaneously and bend the lower note up to the pitch of the higher.

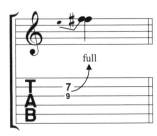

BEND & RESTRIKE: Strike the note and bend as indicated then restrike the string where the symbol occurs.

BEND, HOLD AND RELEASE: Same as bend and release but hold the bend for the duration of the tie.

BEND AND TAP: Bend the note as indicated and tap the higher fret while still holding the bend.

VIBRATO: The string is vibrated by rapidly bending and releasing the note with the fretting hand.

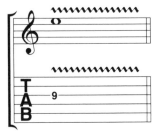

HAMMER-ON: Strike the first note with one finger, then sound the second note (on the same string) with another finger by fretting it without picking.

PULL-OFF: Place both fingers on the notes to be sounded, strike the first note and without picking, pull the finger off to sound the second note.

LEGATO SLIDE (GLISS): Strike the first note and then slide the same fret-hand finger up or down to the second note. The second note is not struck.

NOTE: The speed of any bend is indicated by the music notation and tempo.

SHIFT SLIDE (GLISS & RESTRIKE): Same as legato slide, except the second note is struck.

TRILL: Very rapidly alternate between the notes indicated by continuously hammering on and pulling off.

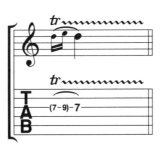

TAPPING: Hammer ("tap") the fret indicated with the pick-hand index or middle finger and pull off to the note fretted by the fret hand.

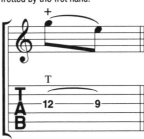

PICK SCRAPE: The edge of the pick is rubbed down (or up) the string, producing a scratchy sound.

MUFFLED STRINGS: A percussive sound is produced by laying the fret hand across the string(s) without depressing, and striking them with the pick hand.

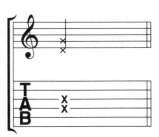

NATURAL HARMONIC: Strike the note while the fret-hand lightly touches the string directly over the fret indicated.

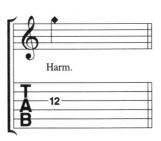

PINCH HARMONIC: The note is fretted normally and a harmonic is produced by adding the edge of the thumb or the tip of the index finger of the pick hand to the normal pick attack.

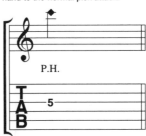

HARP HARMONIC: The note is fretted normally and a harmonic is produced by gently resting the pick hand's index finger directly above the indicated fret (in brackets) while plucking the appropriate string.

PALM MUTING: The note is partially muted by the pick hand lightly touching the string(s) just before the bridge.

RAKE: Drag the pick across the strings indicated with a single motion.

TREMOLO PICKING: The note is picked as rapidly and continuously as possible.

ARPEGGIATE: Play the notes of the chord indicated by quickly rolling them from bottom to top.

SWEEP PICKING: Rhythmic downstroke and/or upstroke motion across the strings.

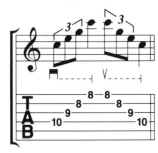

VIBRATO DIVE BAR AND RETURN: The pitch of the note or chord is dropped a specific number of steps (in rhythm) then returned to the original pitch.

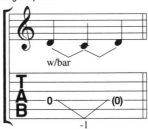

VIBRATO BAR SCOOP: Depress the bar just before striking the note, then quickly release the bar.

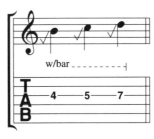

VIBRATO BAR DIP: Strike the note and then immediately drop a specific number of steps, then release back to the original pitch.

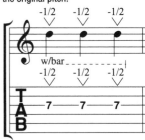

Additional Musical Definitions

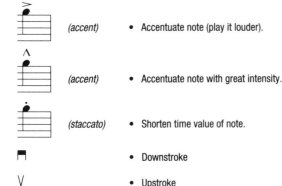

(accent) • Accentuate note (play it louder).

(accent) • Accentuate note with great intensity.

(staccato) • Shorten time value of note.

• Downstroke

V • Upstroke

NOTE: Tablature numbers in brackets mean:
1. The note is sustained, but a new articulation (such as hammer on or slide) begins.
2. A note may be fretted but not necessarily played.

D.%. al Coda

D.C. al Fine

tacet

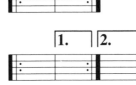

| 1. | 2. |

• Go back to the sign (%), then play until the bar marked *To Coda* ⊕ then skip to the section marked ⊕ *Coda*.

• Go back to the beginning of the song and play until the bar marked *Fine*.

• Instrument is silent (drops out).

• Repeat bars between signs.

• When a repeated section has different endings, play the first ending only the first time and the second ending only the second time.

Politik

Words & Music by Guy Berryman, Jon Buckland, Will Champion & Chris Martin

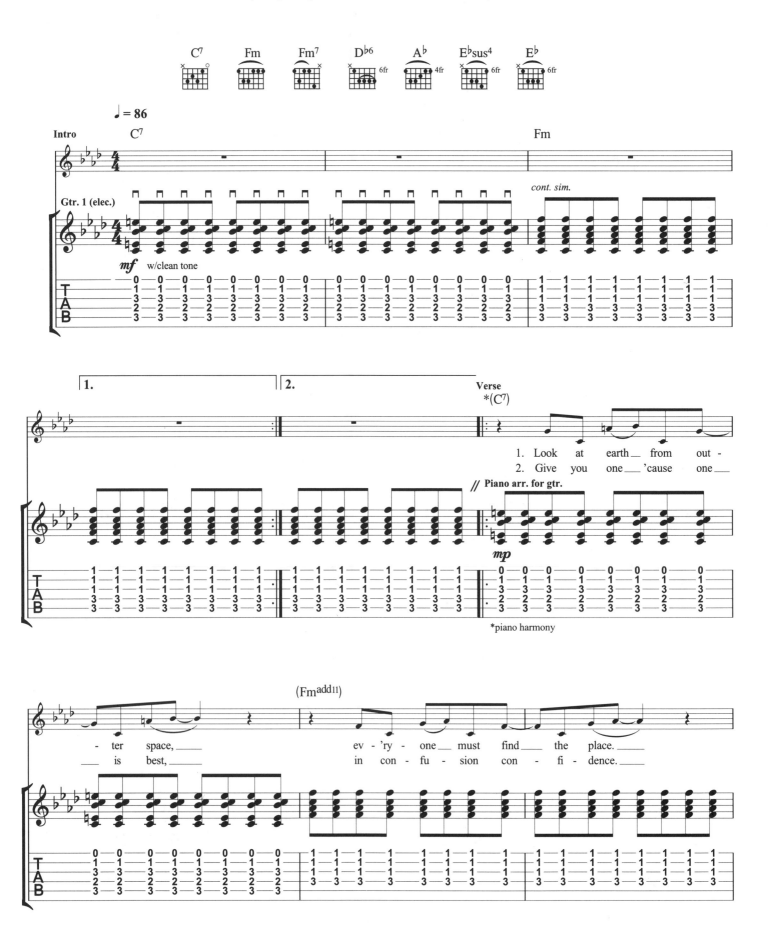

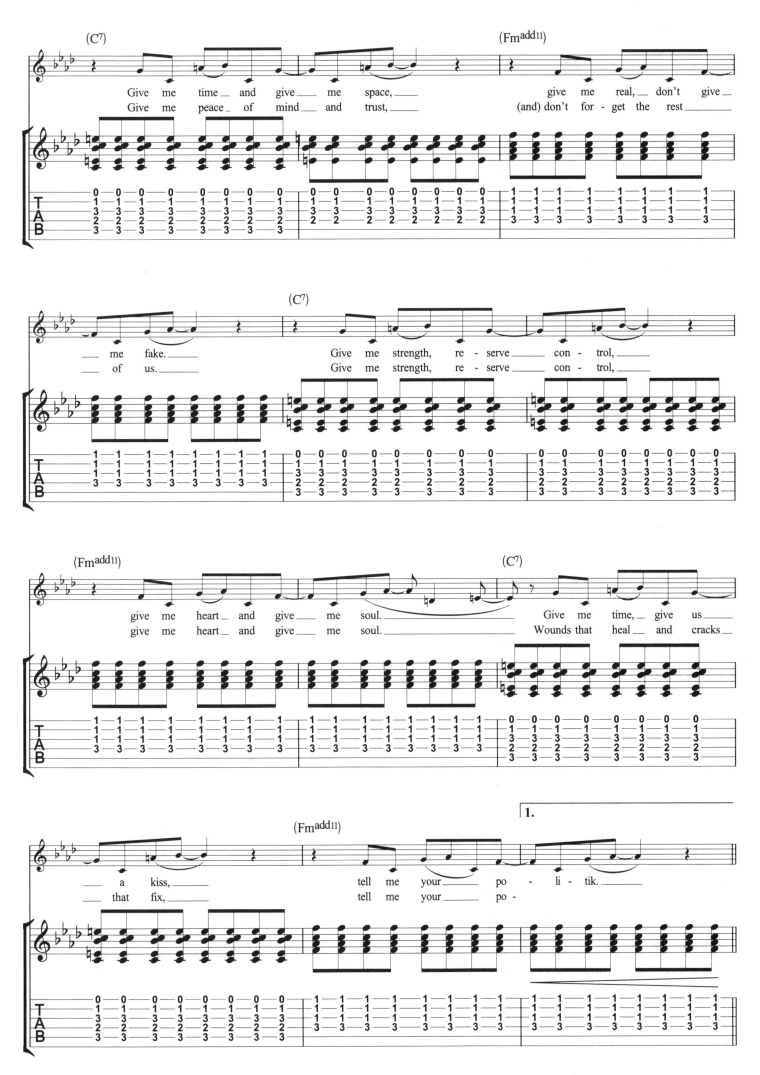

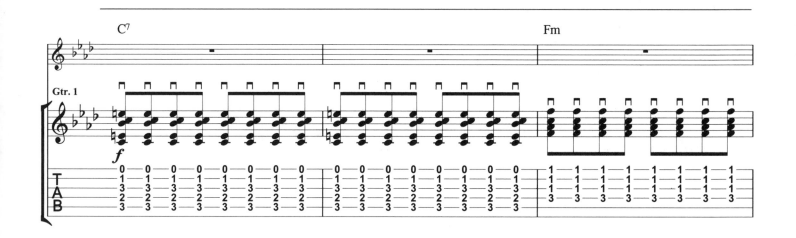

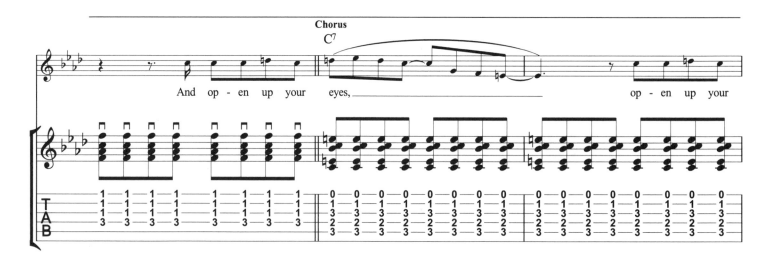

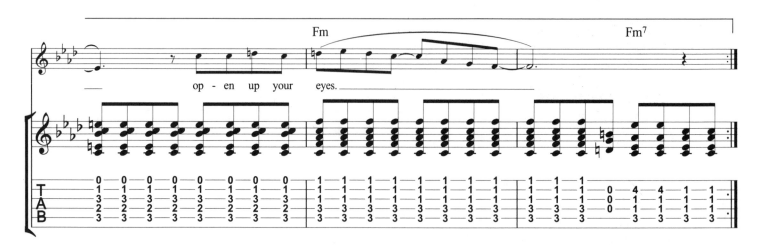

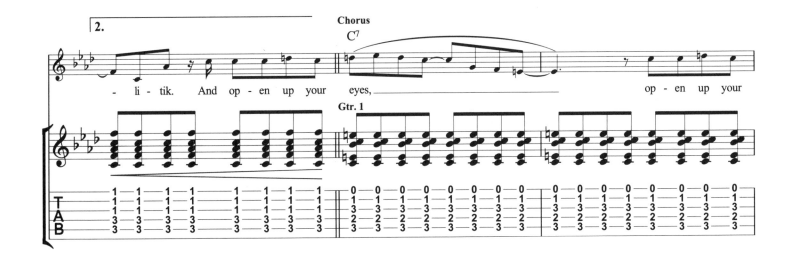

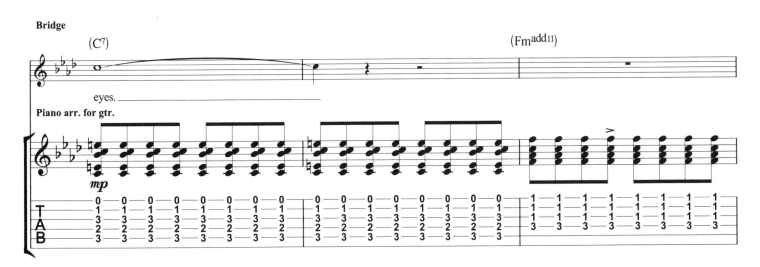

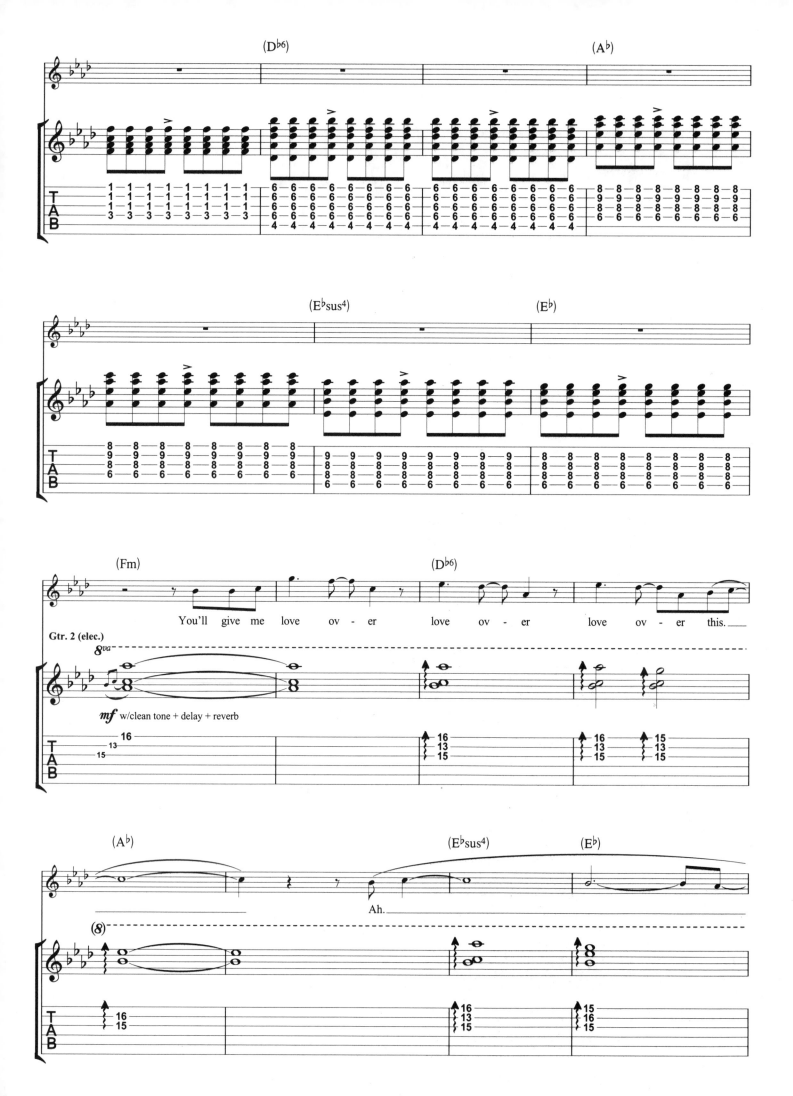

In My Place

Words & Music by Guy Berryman, Jon Buckland, Will Champion & Chris Martin

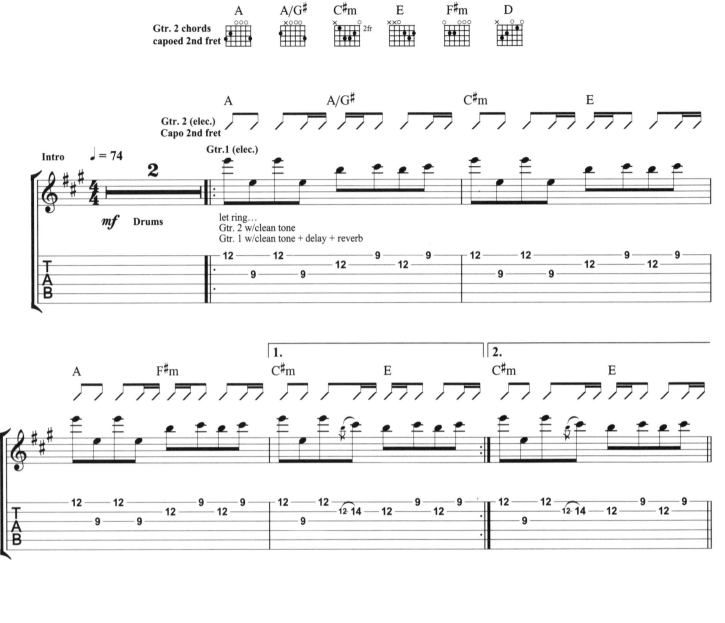

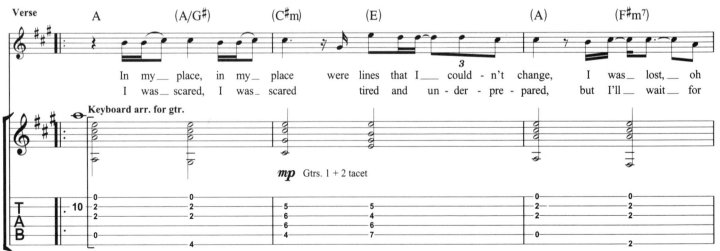

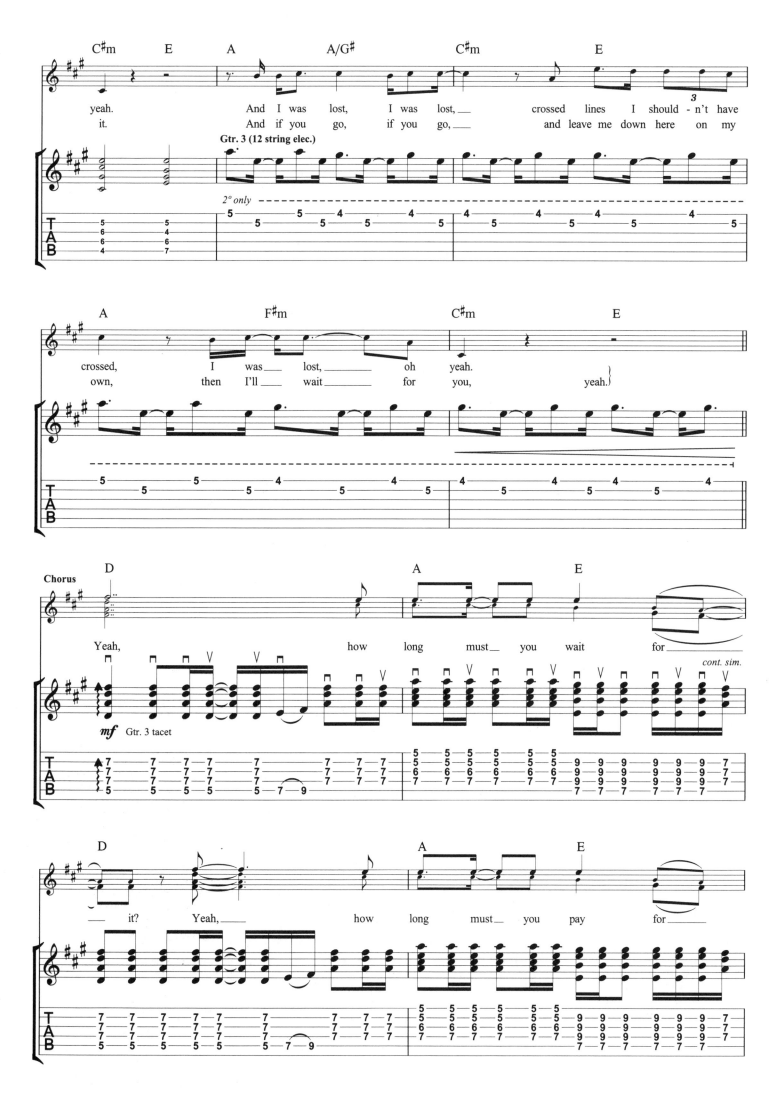

15

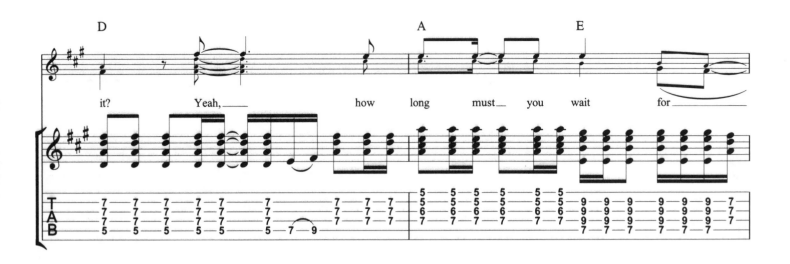

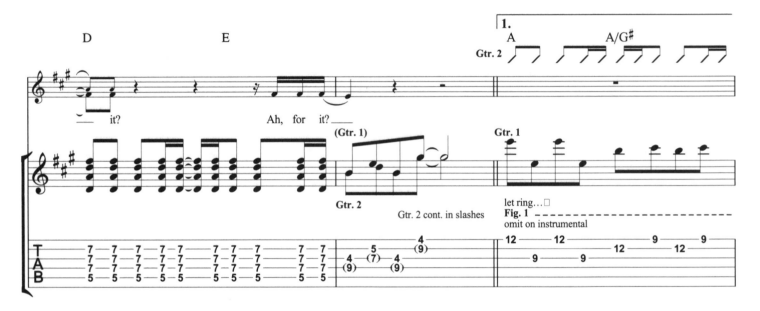

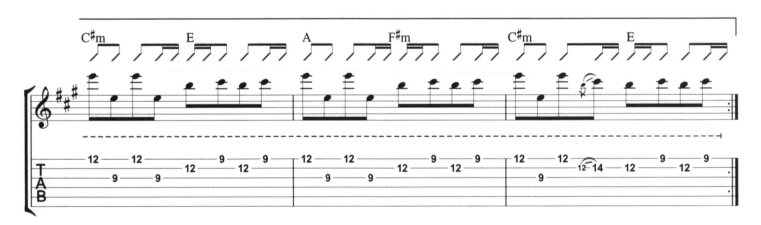

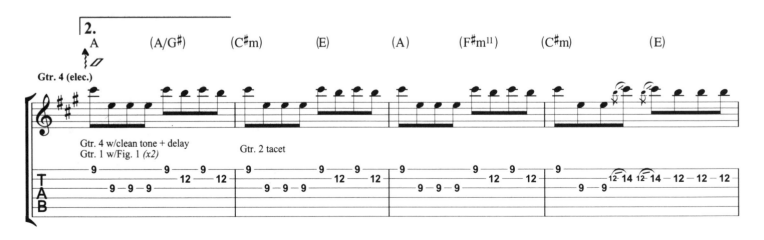

God Put A Smile Upon Your Face

Words & Music by Guy Berryman, Jon Buckland, Will Champion & Chris Martin

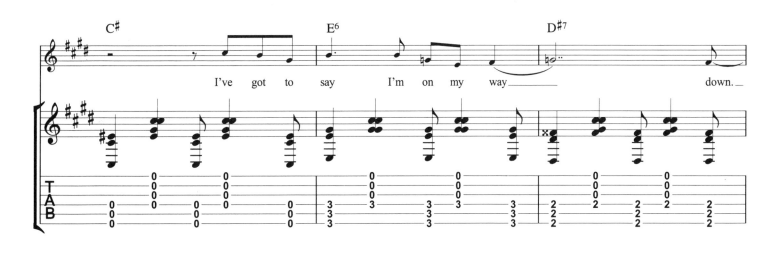

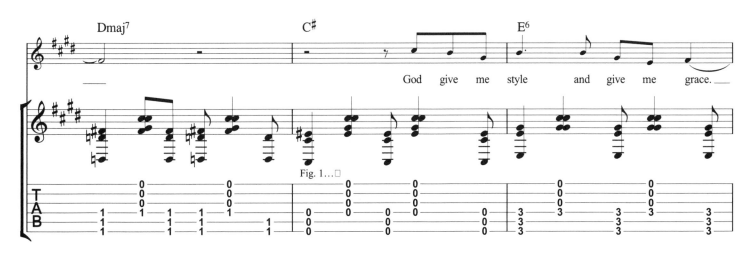

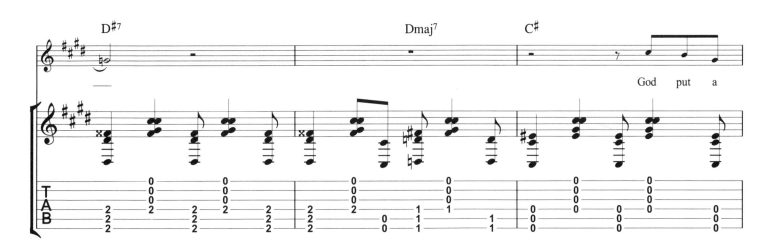

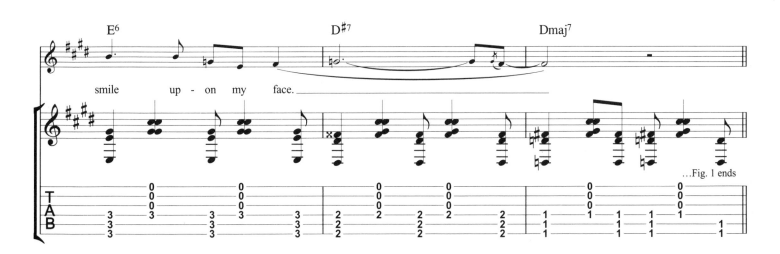

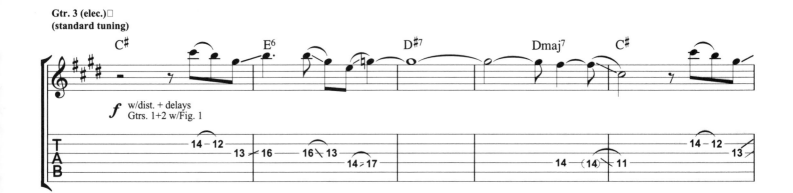

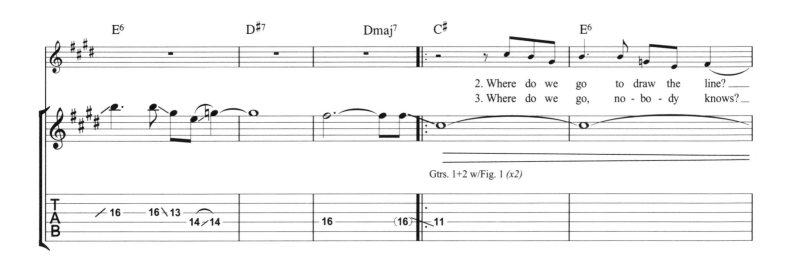

2. Where do we go to draw the line? ___
3. Where do we go, no - bo - dy knows? ___

Gtrs. 1+2 w/Fig. 1 *(x2)*

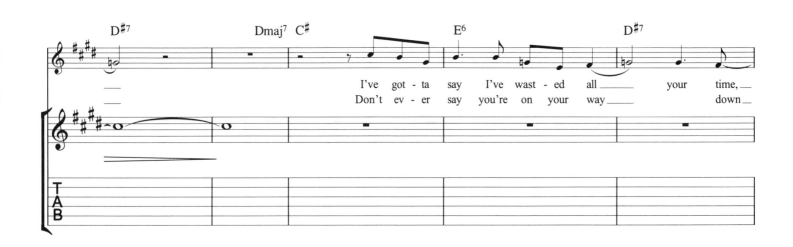

I've got - ta say I've wast - ed all ___ your time, ___
Don't ev - er say you're on your way ___ down ___

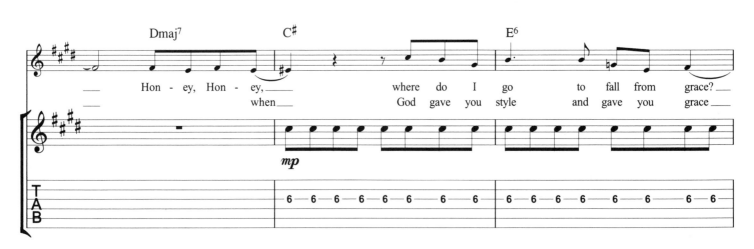

___ Hon - ey, Hon - ey, ___ where do I go to fall from grace? ___
___ when ___ God gave you style and gave you grace ___

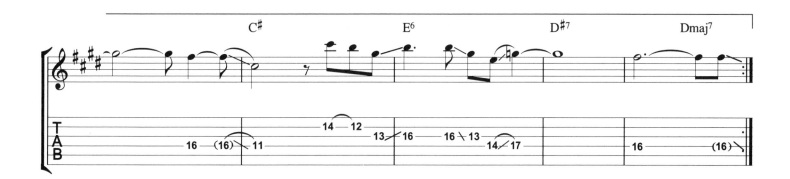

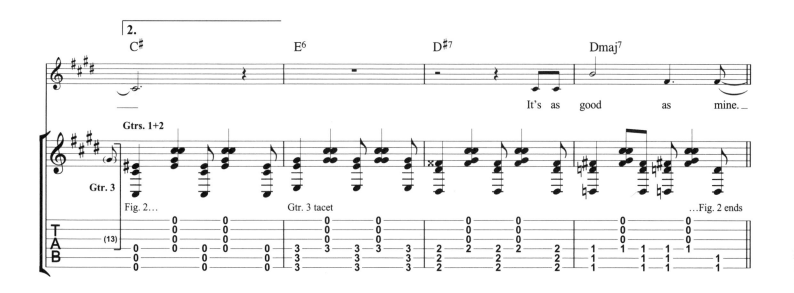

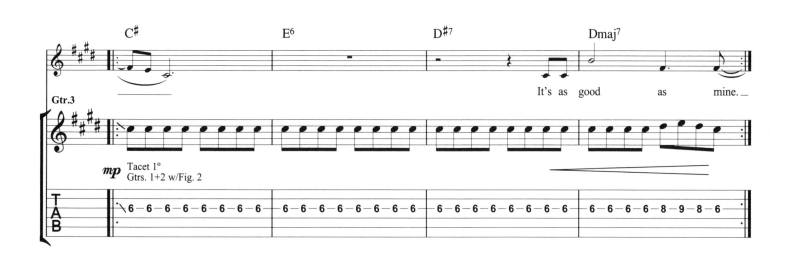

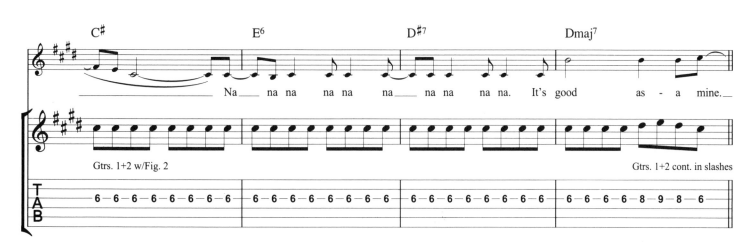

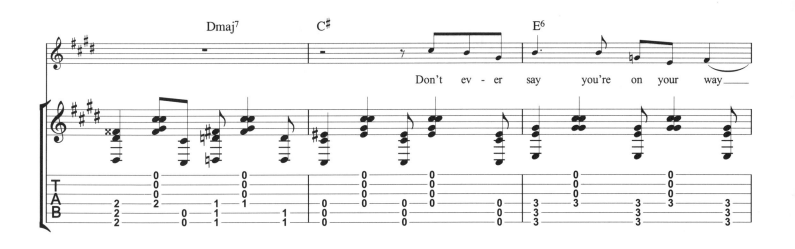

Don't ev - er say you're on your way

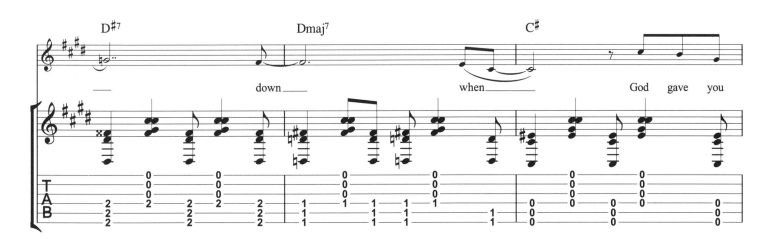

— down ____ when ____ God gave you

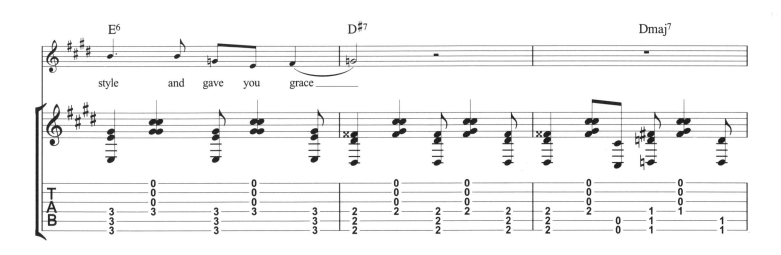

style and gave you grace ____

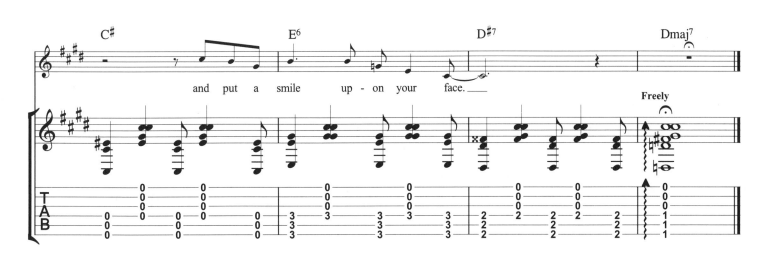

and put a smile up - on your face. ____

The Scientist

Words & Music by Guy Berryman, Jon Buckland, Will Champion & Chris Martin

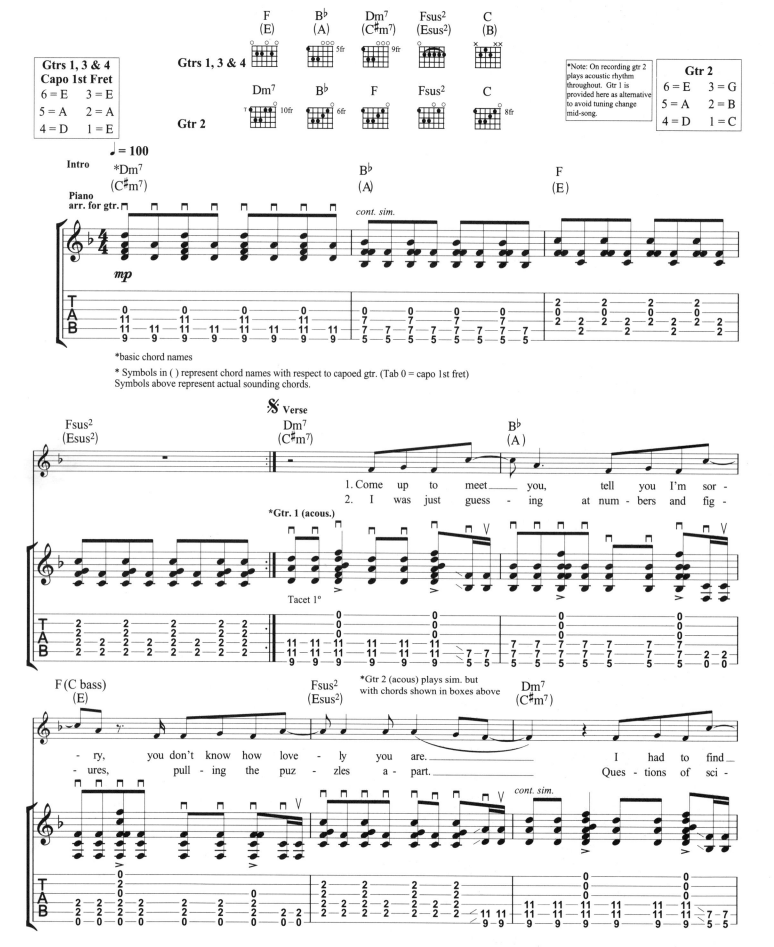

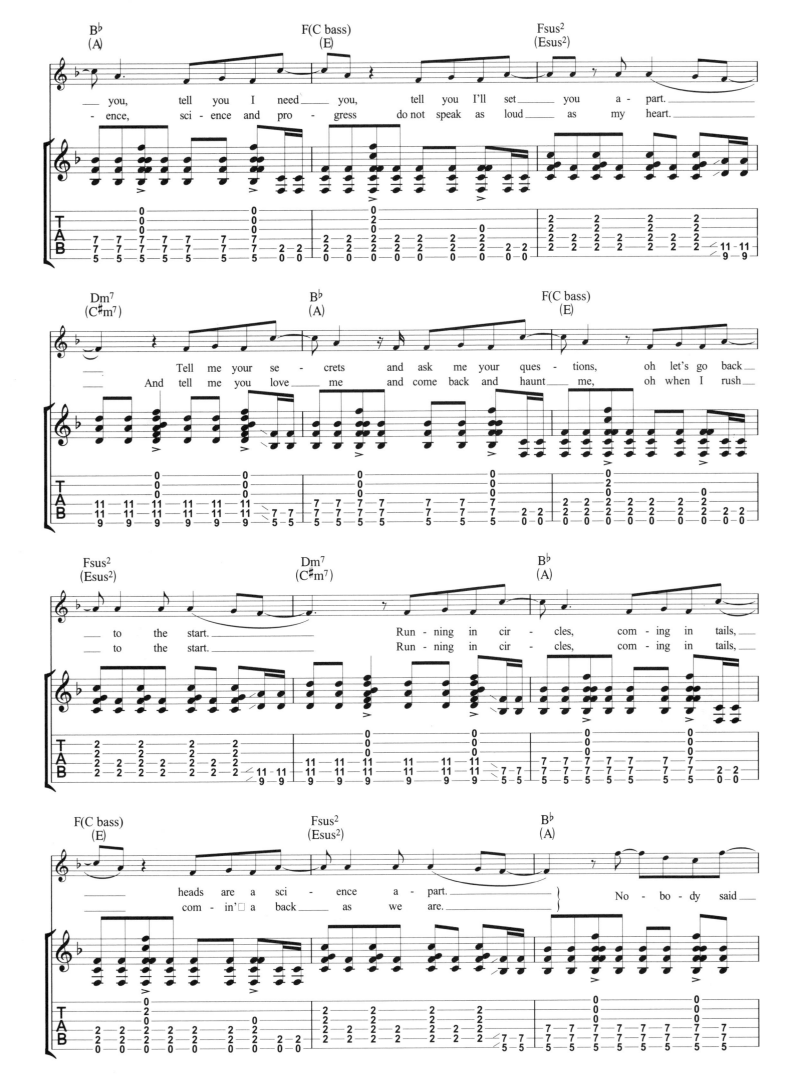

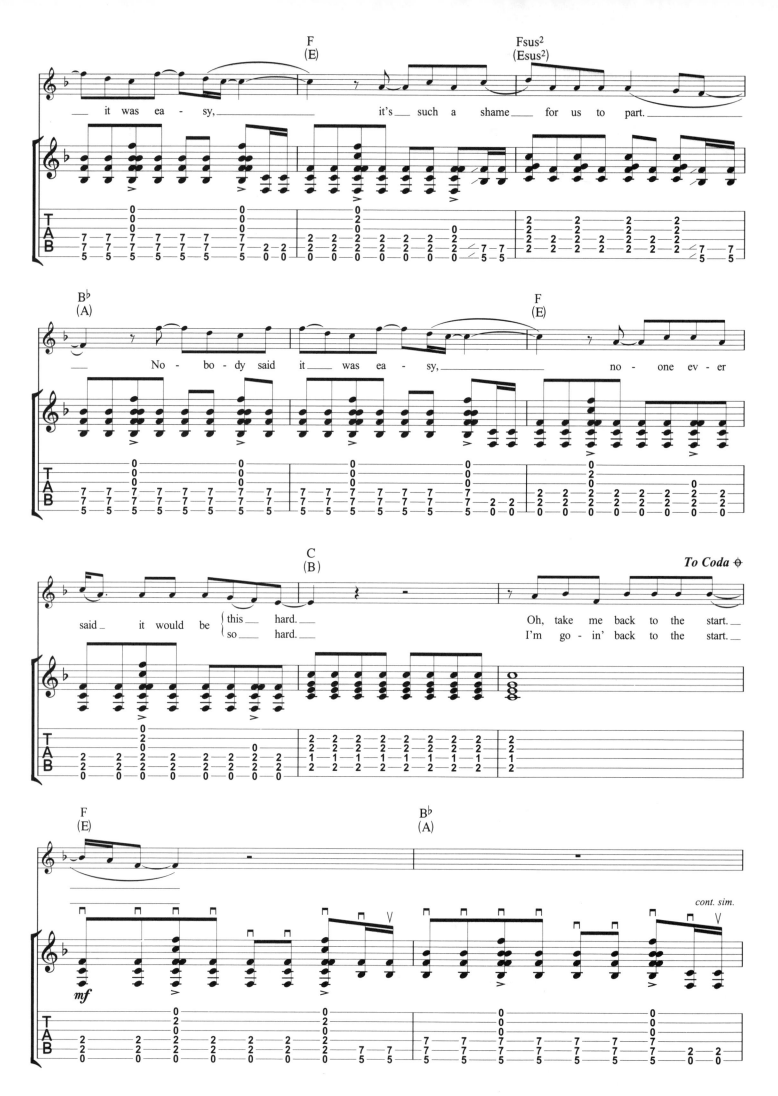

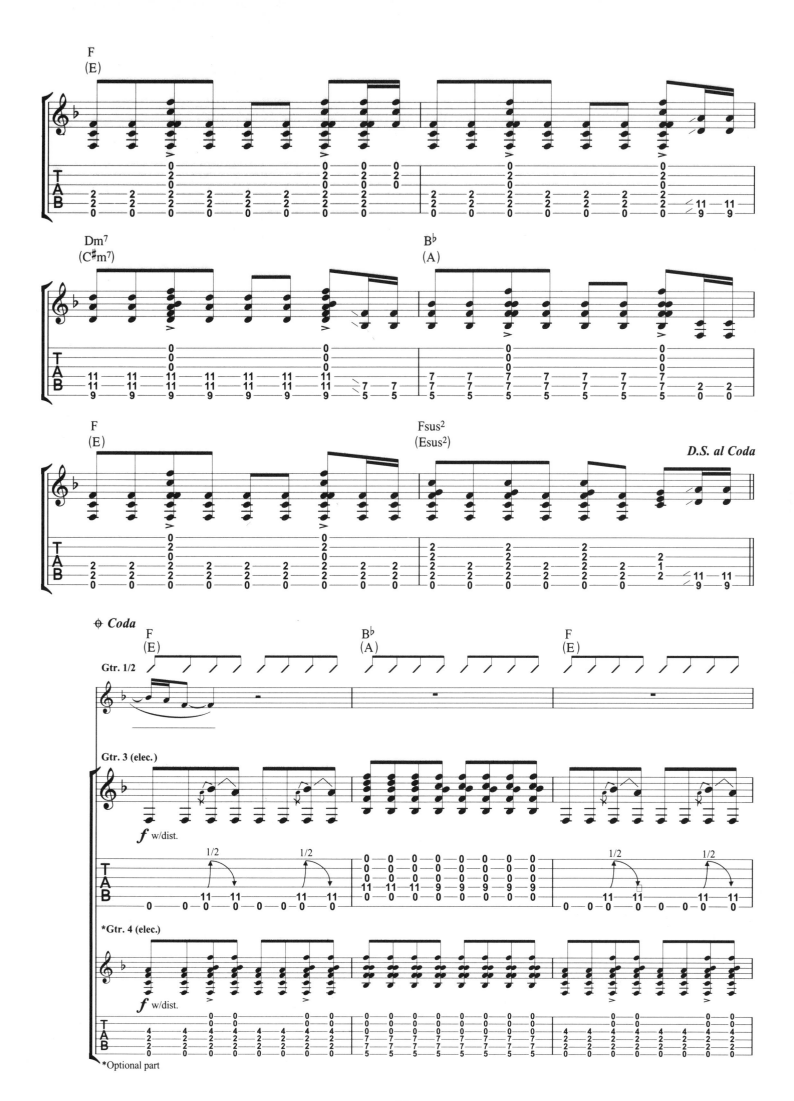

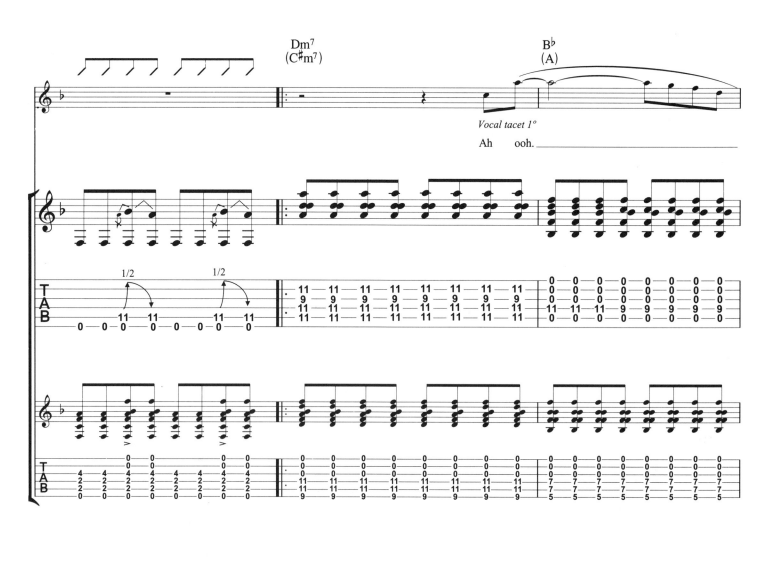

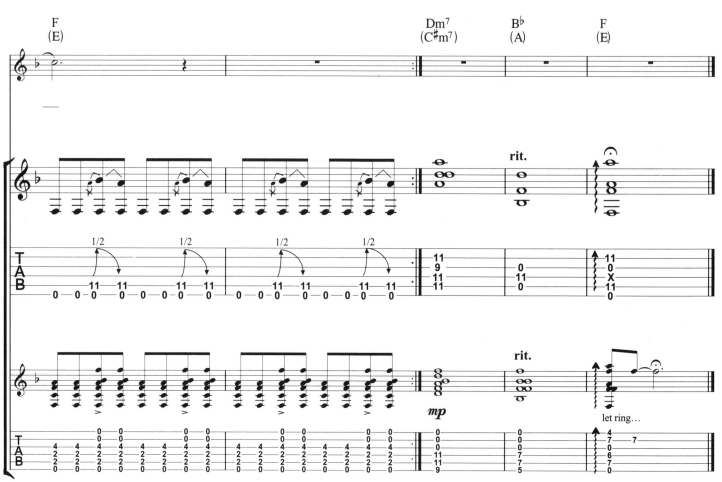

30

Clocks

Words & Music by Guy Berryman, Jon Buckland, Will Champion & Chris Martin

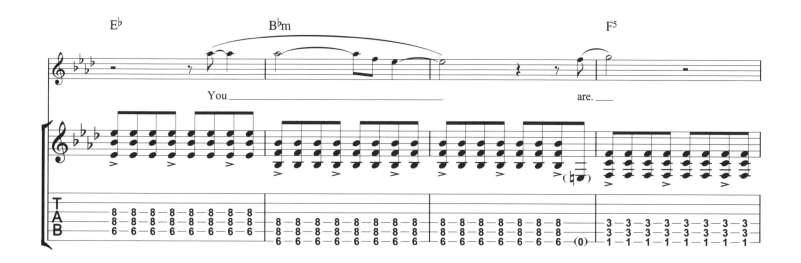

You _____ are. ___

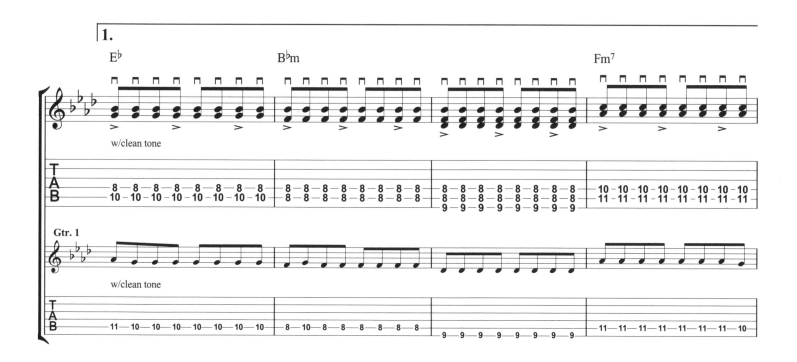

1.

w/clean tone

Gtr. 1

w/clean tone

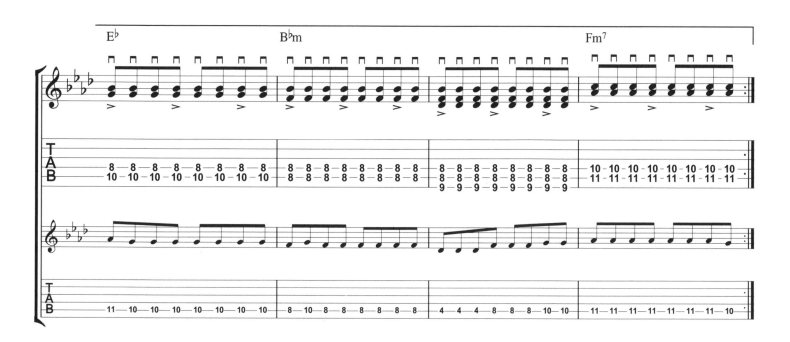

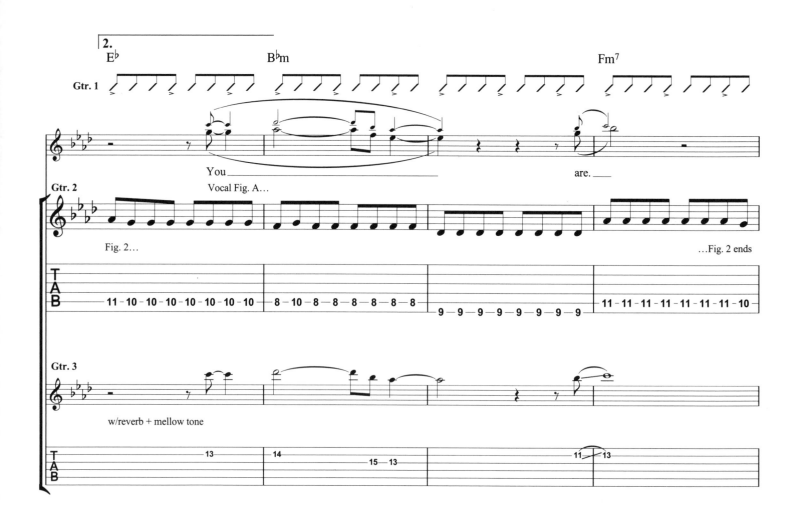

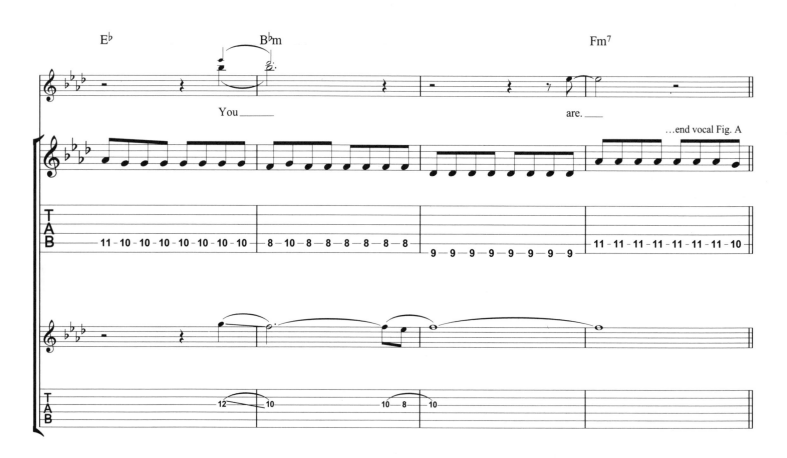

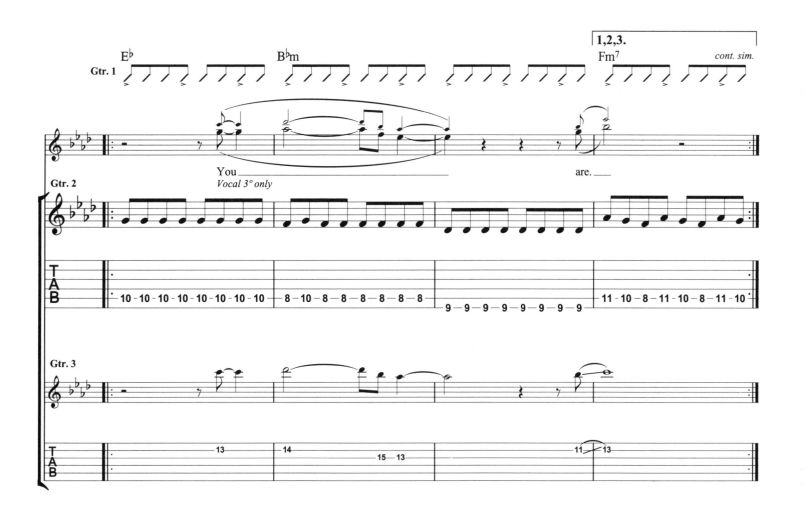

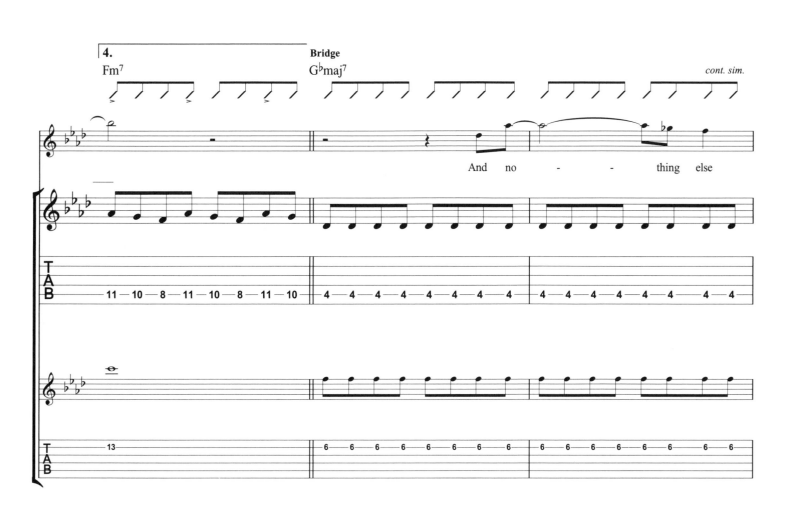

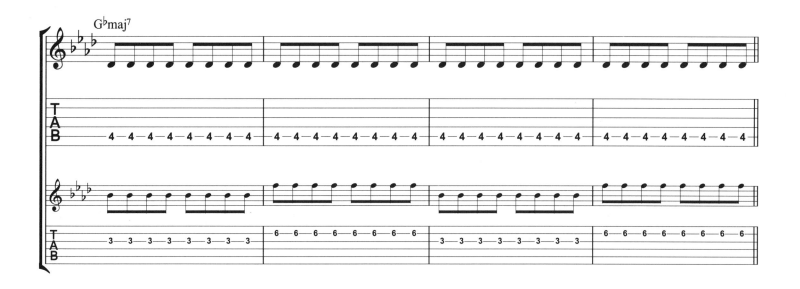

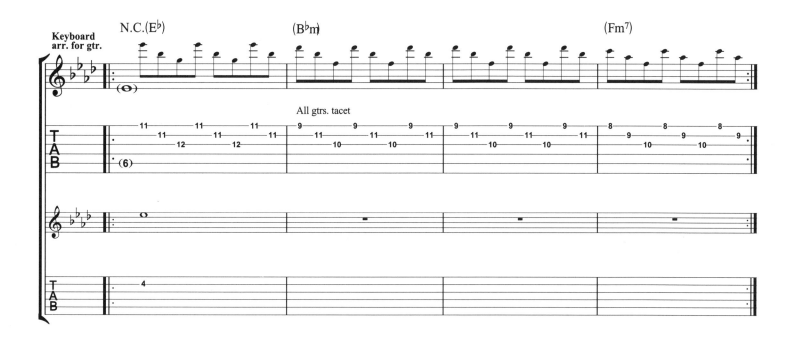

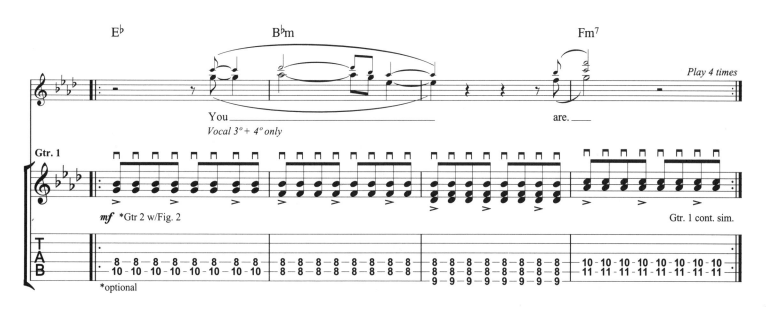

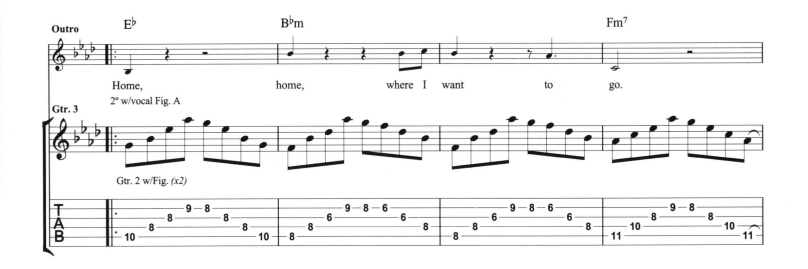

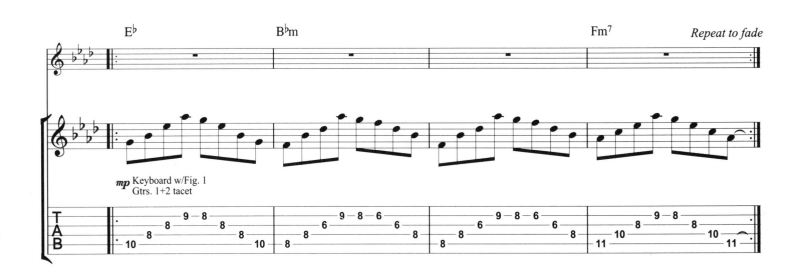

Daylight

Words & Music by Guy Berryman, Jon Buckland, Will Champion & Chris Martin

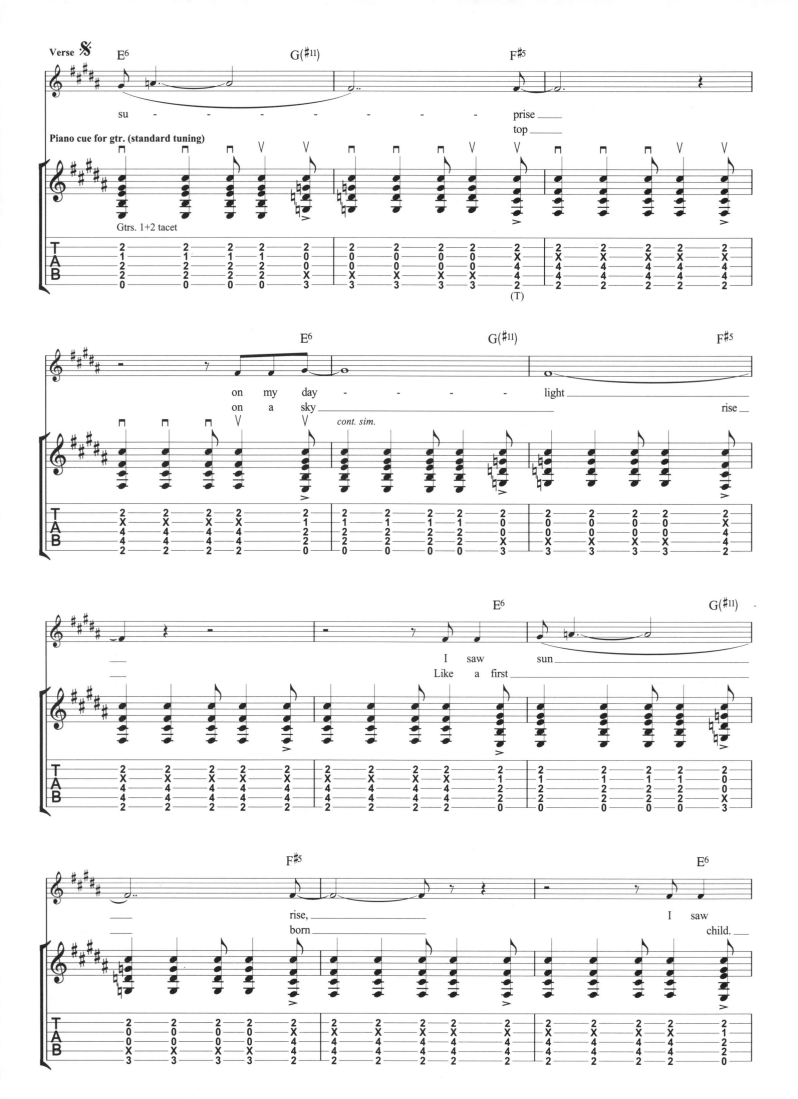

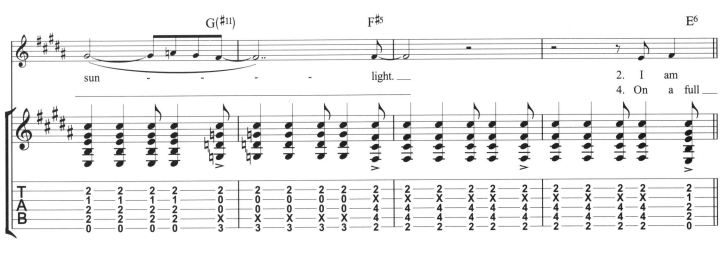

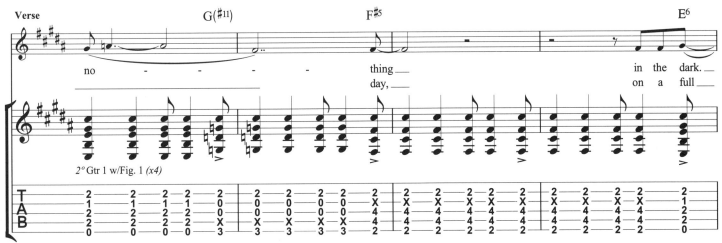

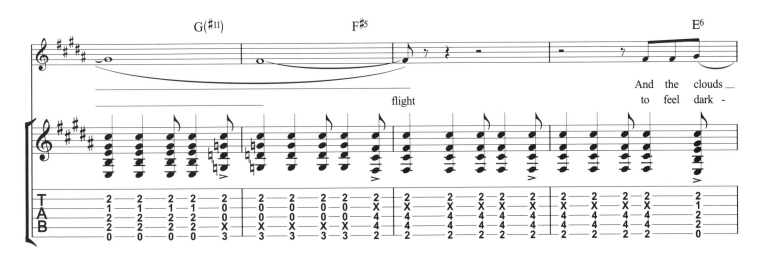

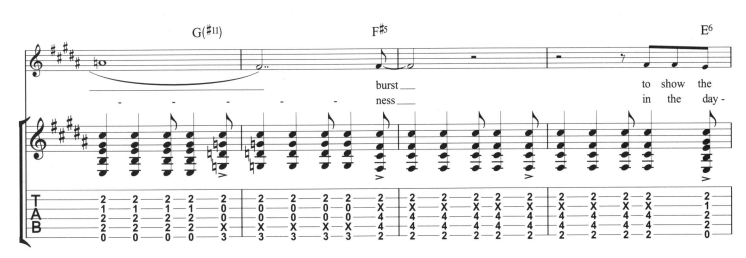

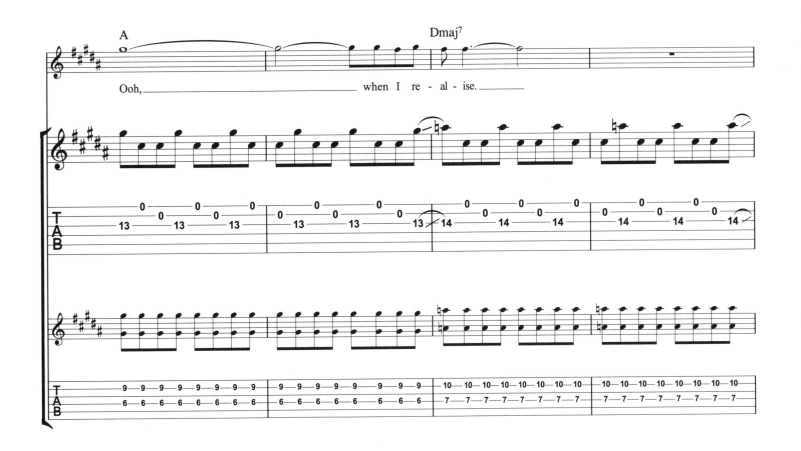

Ooh,_____ when I re - al - ise.____

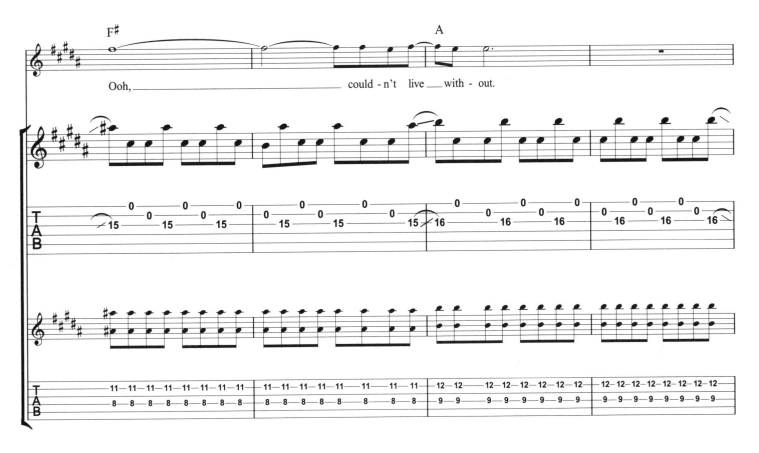

Ooh,_____ could - n't live ___ with - out.

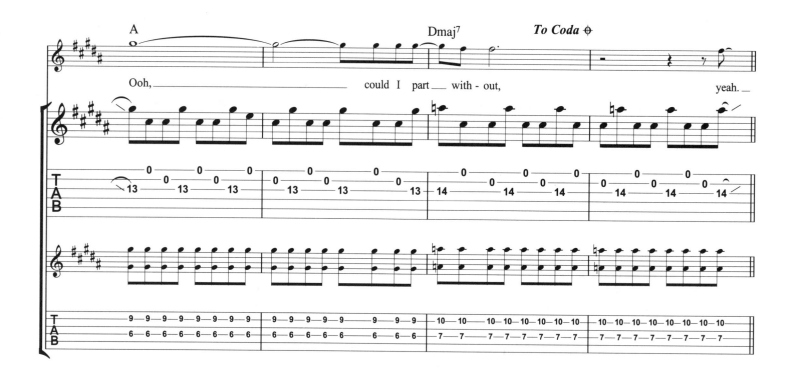

Ooh,_____ could I part___ with - out, _____ yeah.___

3. On a hill -

Green Eyes

Words & Music by Guy Berryman, Jon Buckland, Will Champion & Chris Martin

49

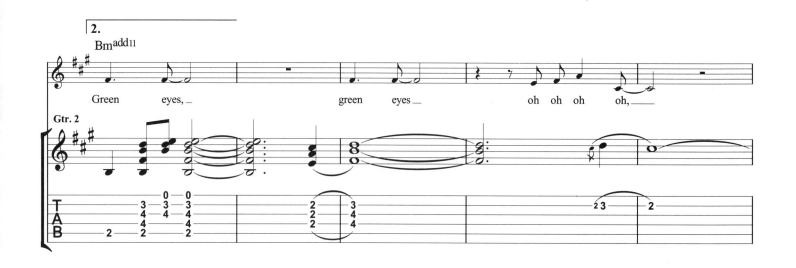

Green eyes, __ green eyes __ oh oh oh oh, __

oh oh oh oh, __ oh oh oh oh, __ oh oh oh oh. __

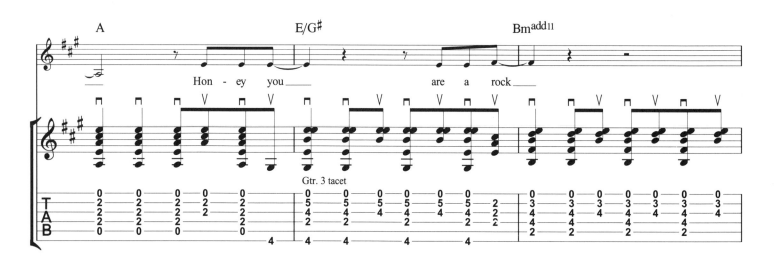

Hon - ey you ____ are a rock ____

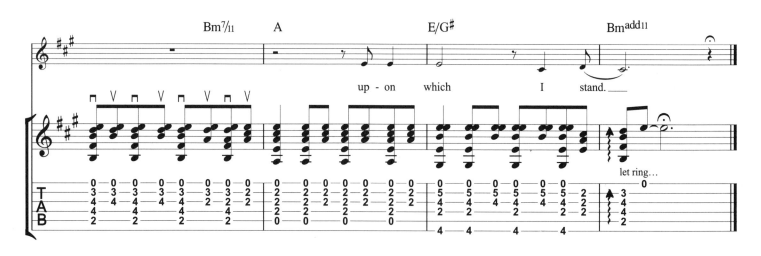

up - on which I stand. ____

Warning Sign

Words & Music by Guy Berryman, Jon Buckland, Will Champion & Chris Martin

* composite part

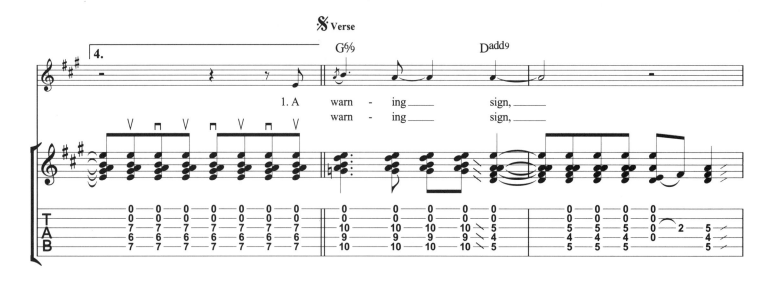

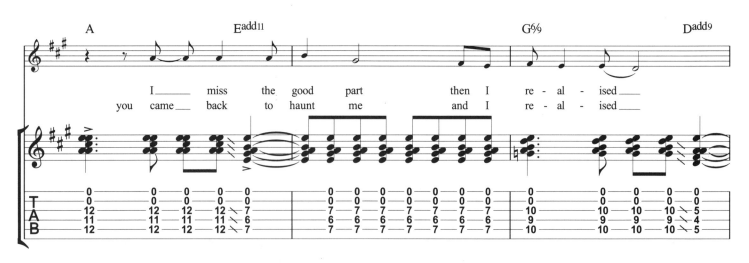

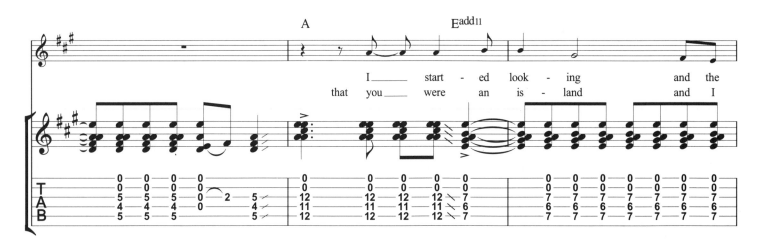

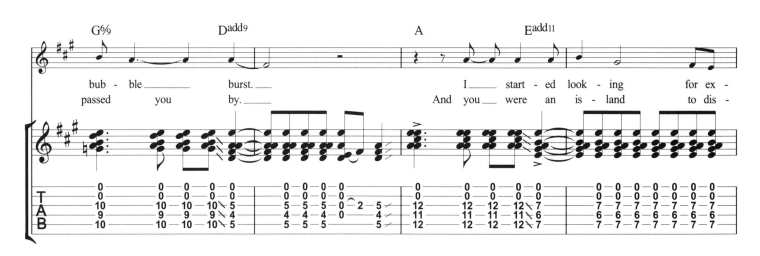

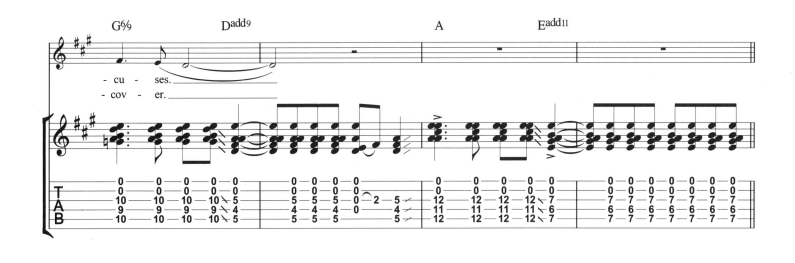

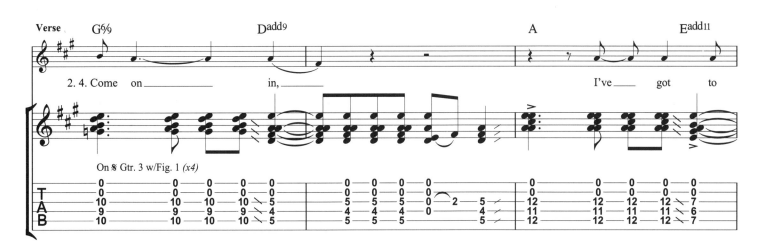

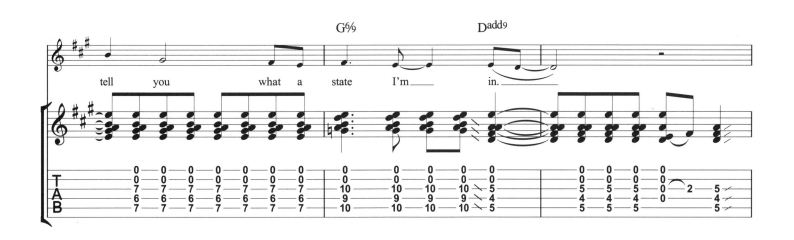

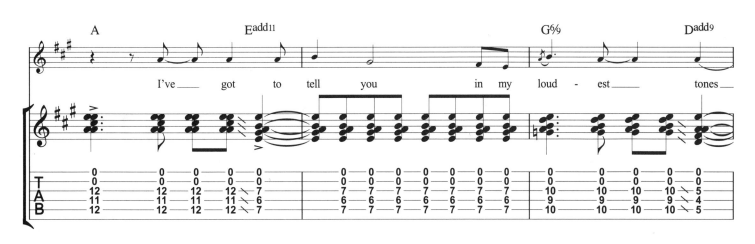

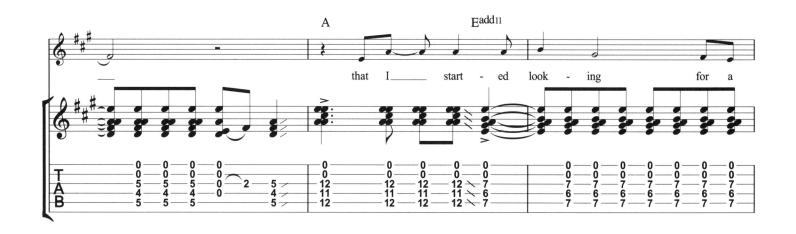

that I ____ start - ed look - ing ____ for a

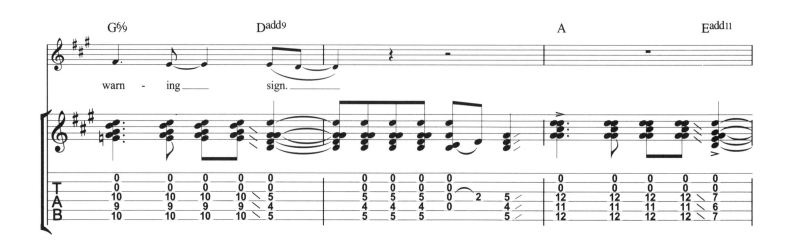

warn - ing ____ sign. ____

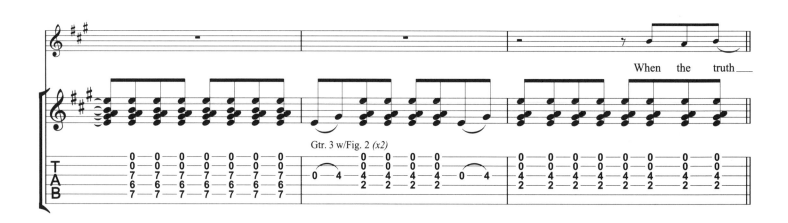

Gtr. 3 w/Fig. 2 *(x2)*

When the truth ____

Chorus

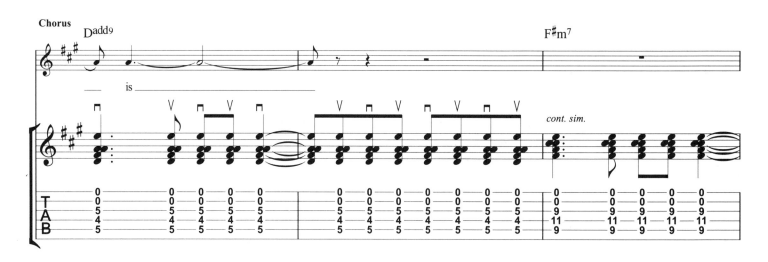

____ is ____

cont. sim.

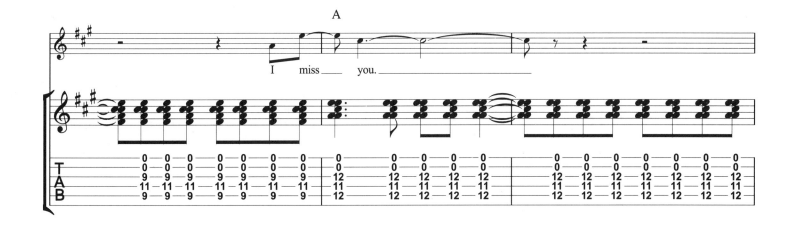

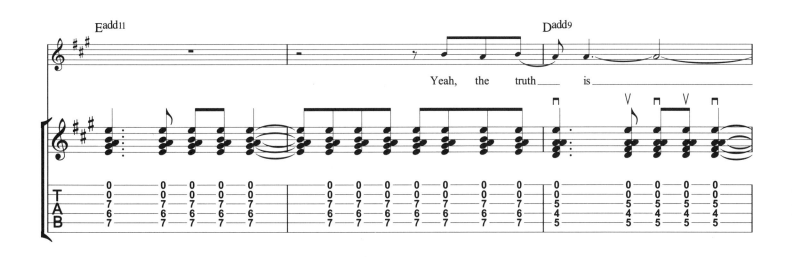

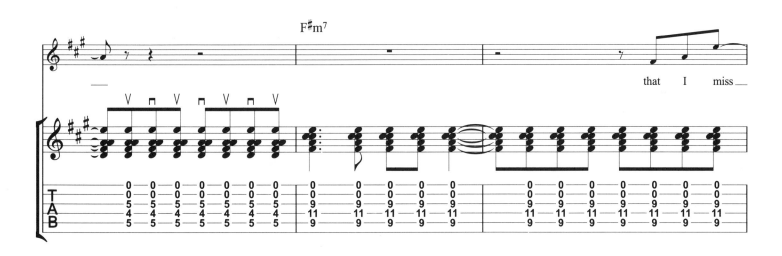

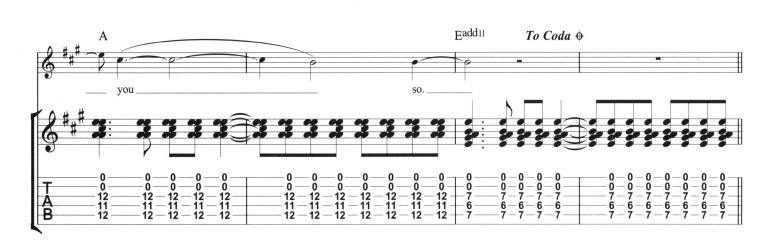

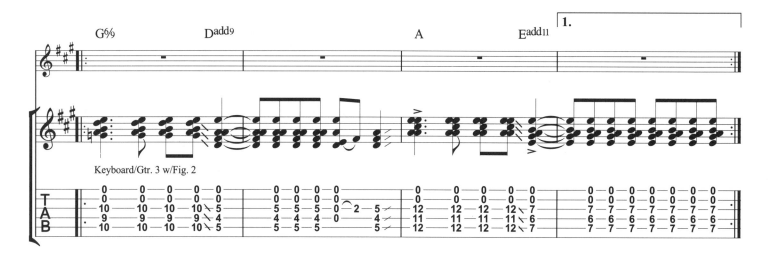

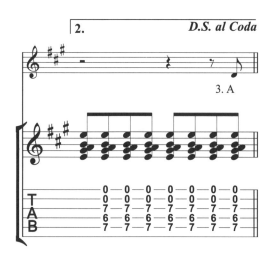

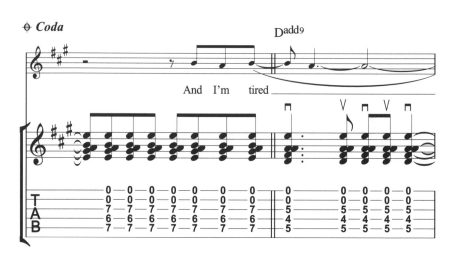

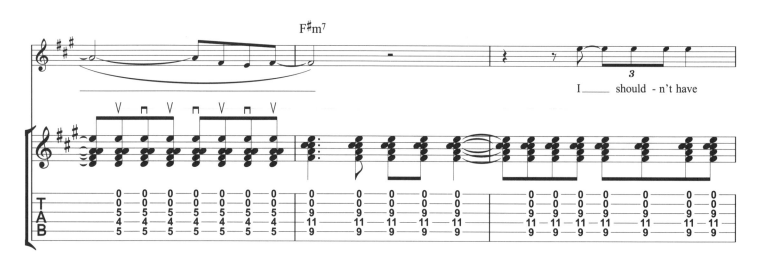

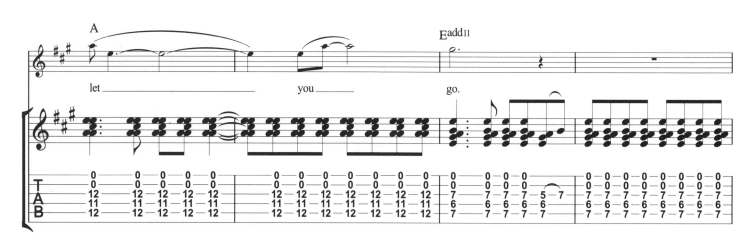

A Whisper

Words & Music by Guy Berryman, Jon Buckland, Will Champion & Chris Martin

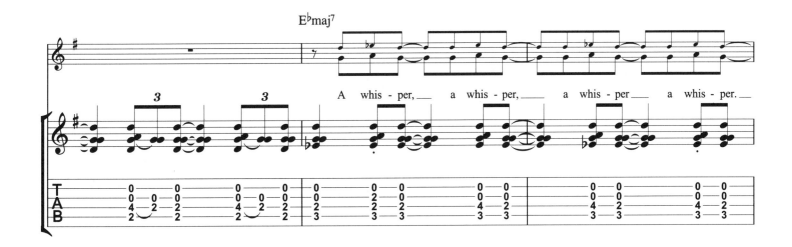

E♭maj7

A whis-per,___ a whis-per,___ a whis-per___ a whis-per.___

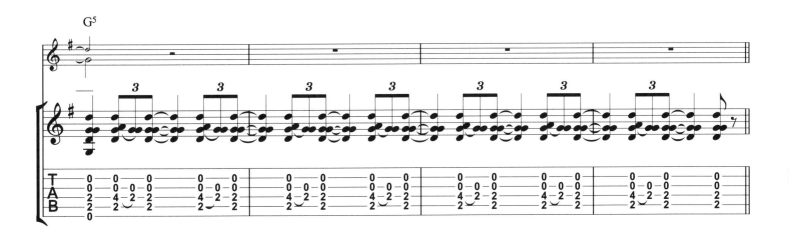

G5

Verse 𝄋

Csus4   C   Csus4   C   Csus4   C

I hear the sound___ of the tick-ing of clocks, re - mem - ber your face so re-

Gtr. 1

(optional)

Gtr. 2 (elec.)

f w/clean tone

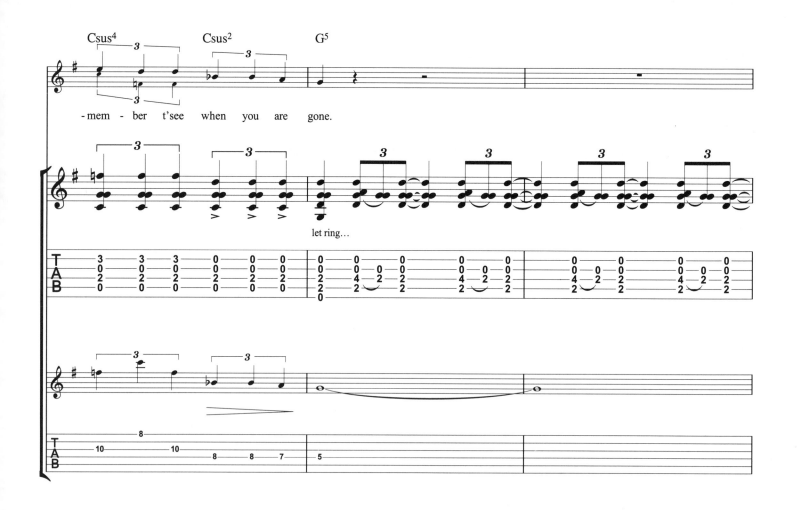

-mem - ber t'see when you are gone.

let ring…

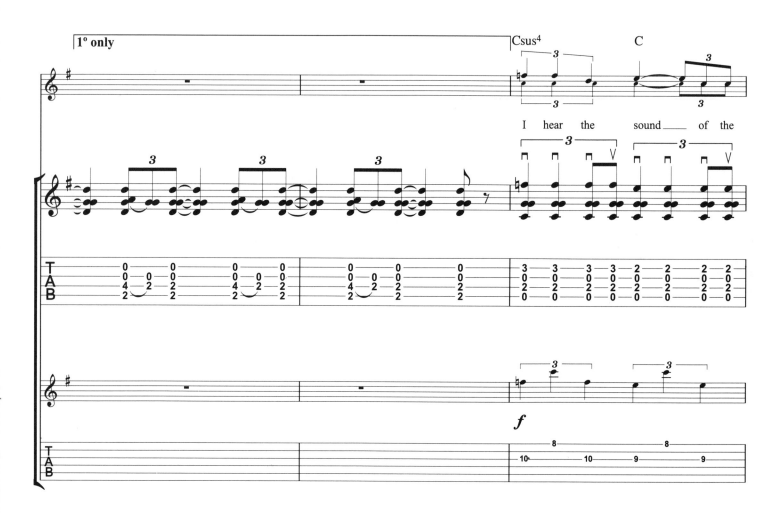

1° only

I hear the sound—— of the

f

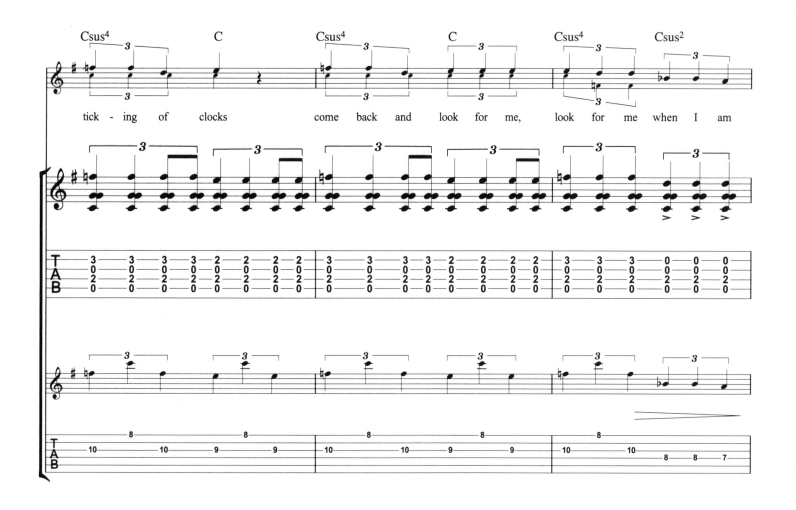

tick - ing of clocks   come back and look for me,   look for me when I am

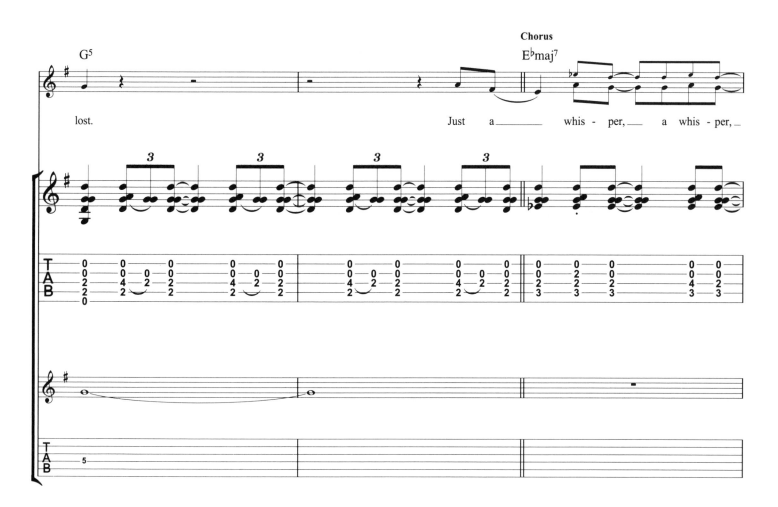

lost.   Just a_____ whis - per,____ a whis - per,____

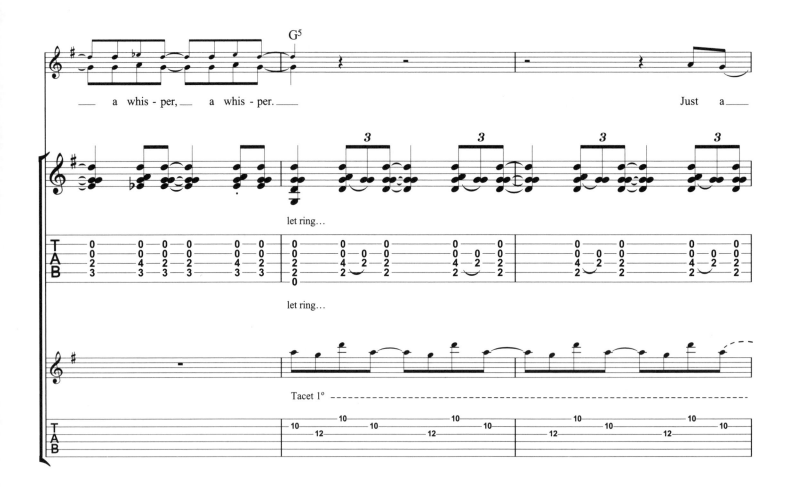

a whis - per,   a whis - per.   Just   a

let ring…

let ring…

Tacet 1°

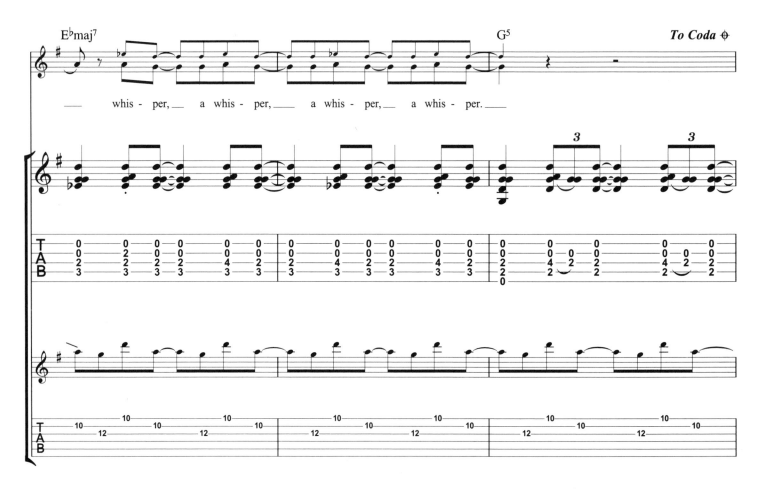

whis - per,   a whis - per,   a whis - per,   a whis - per.

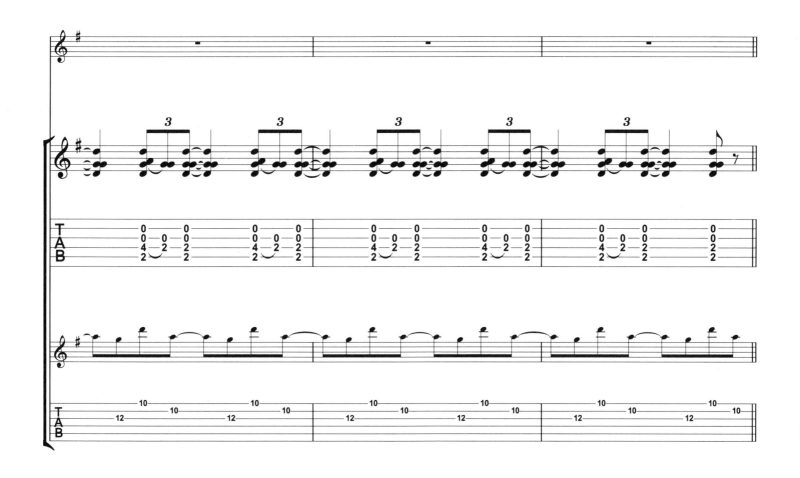

Bridge

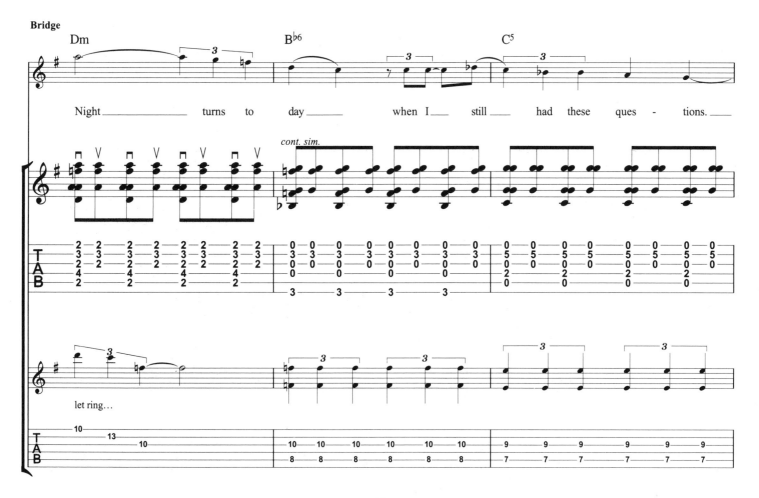

Night _____ turns to day _____ when I ___ still ___ had these ques - tions. _____

let ring...

63

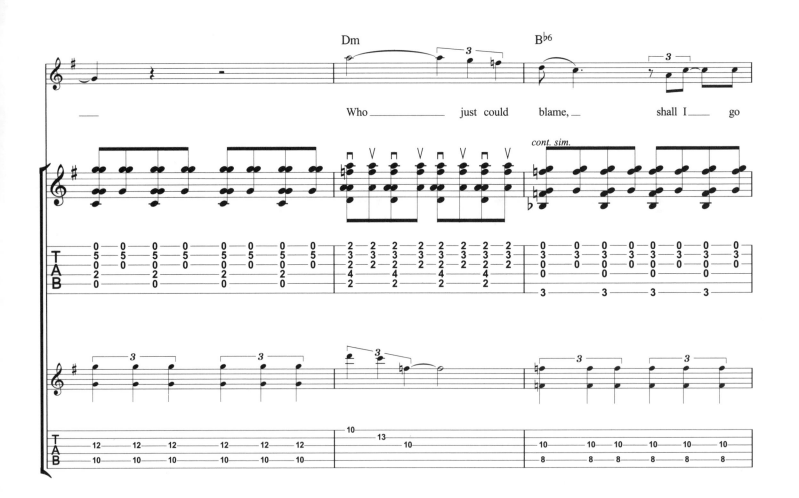

Who _____ just could blame, ___ shall I ___ go

for - wards or back - wards? _____ And not _____ since to -

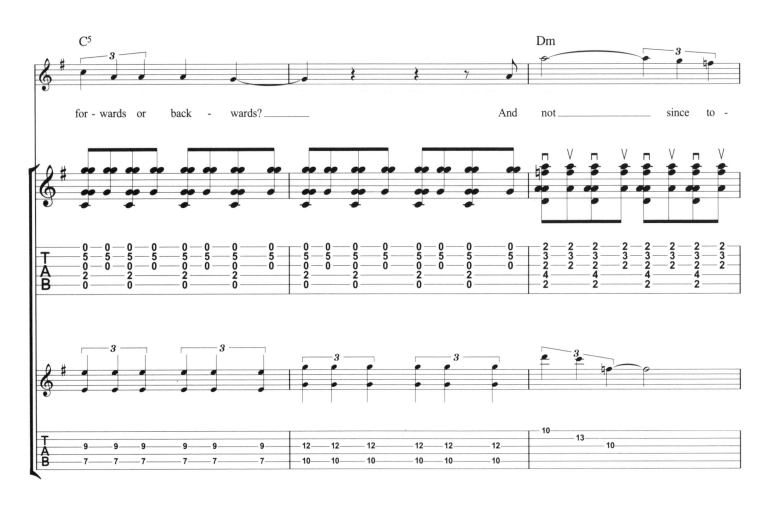

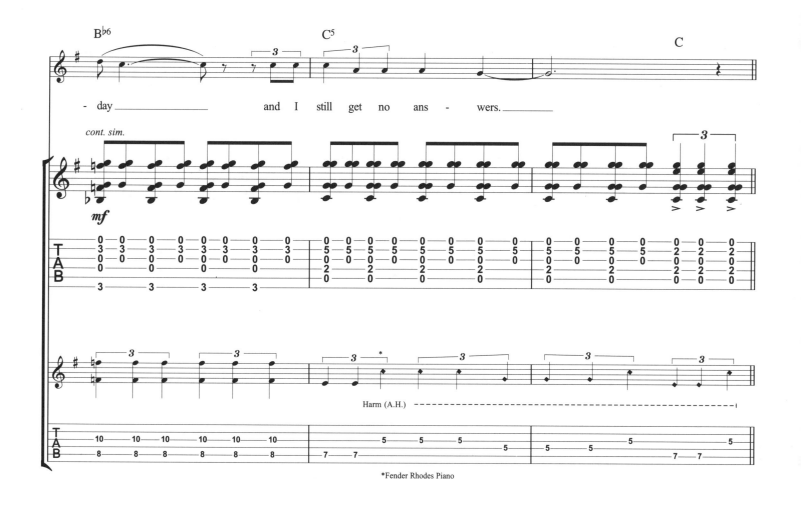

*Fender Rhodes Piano

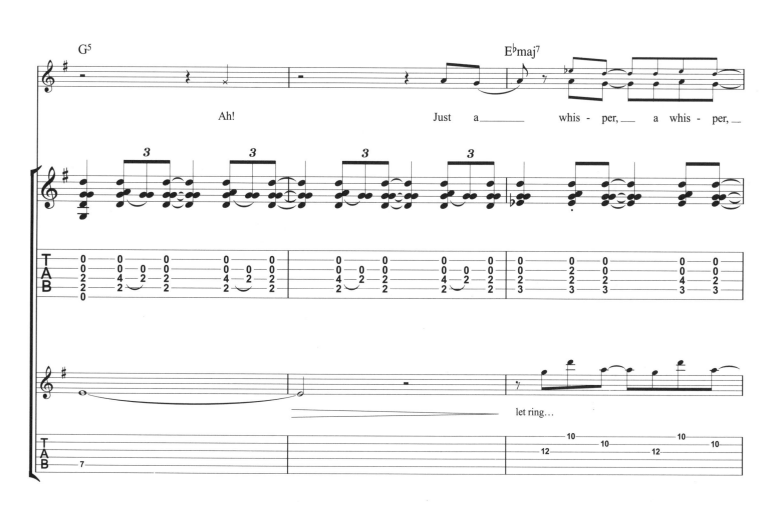

let ring…

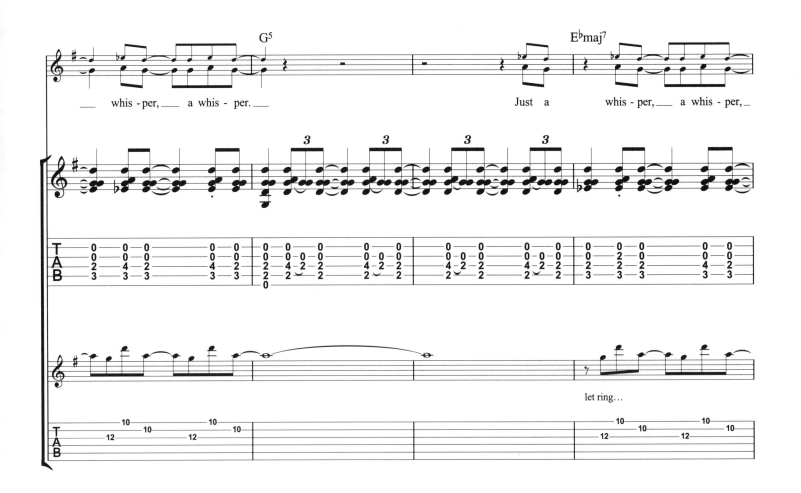

whis - per, ___ a whis - per. ___   Just a   whis - per, ___ a whis - per, ___

let ring...

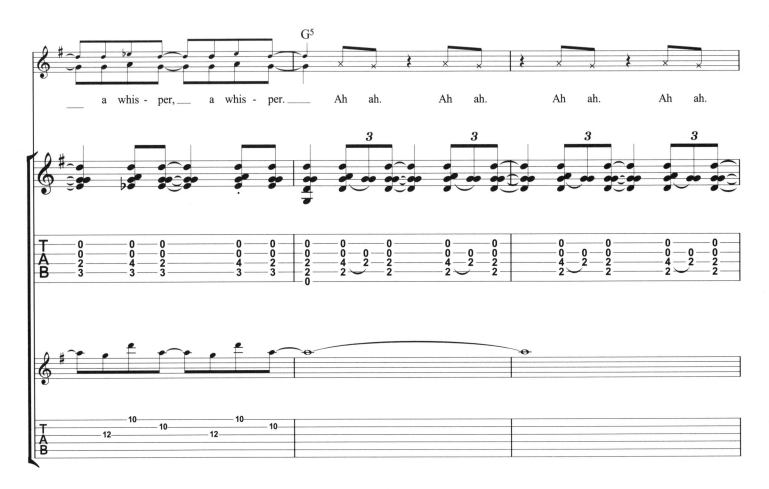

___ a whis - per, ___ a whis - per. ___ Ah ah.   Ah ah.   Ah ah.   Ah ah.

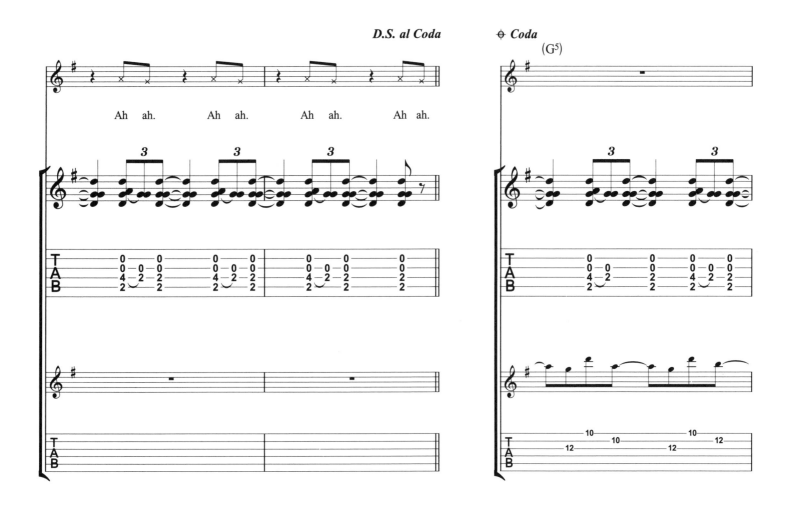

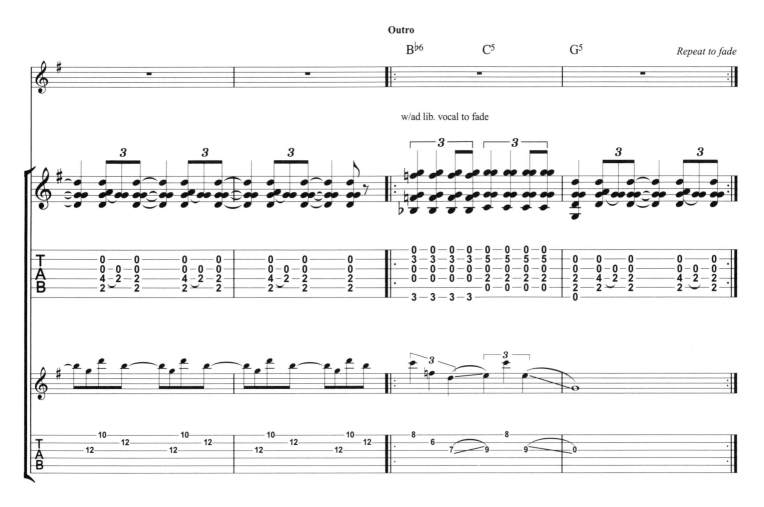

A Rush Of Blood To The Head

Words & Music by Guy Berryman, Jon Buckland, Will Champion & Chris Martin

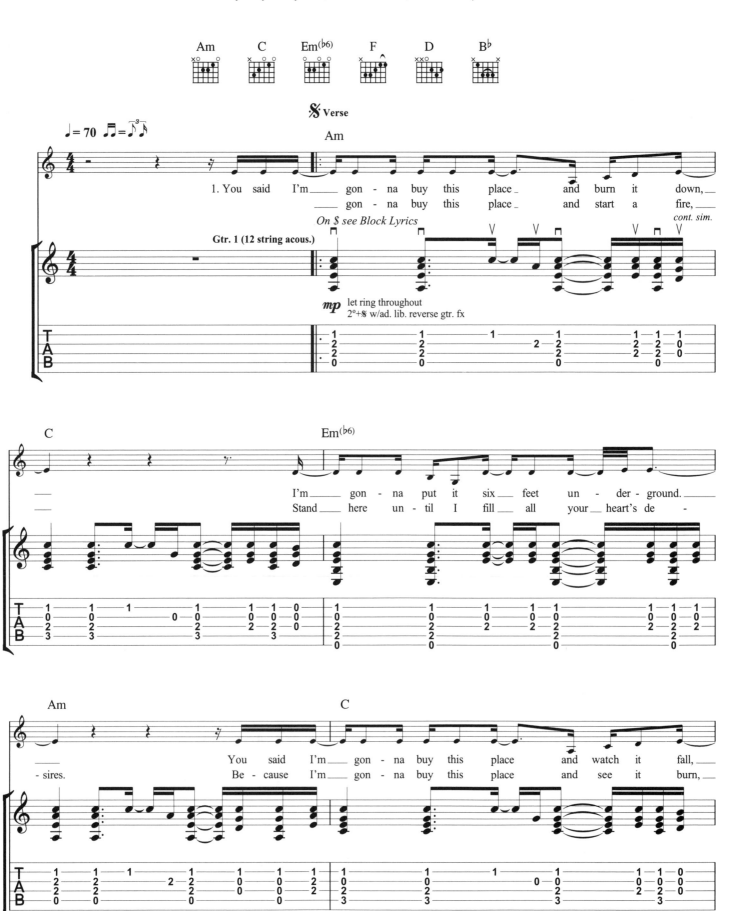

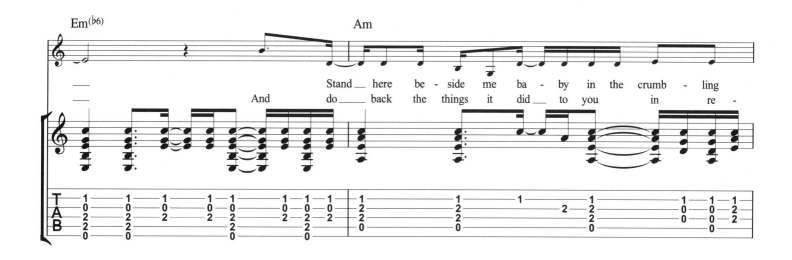

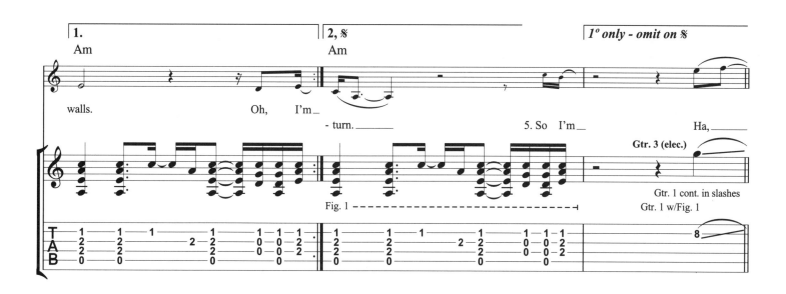

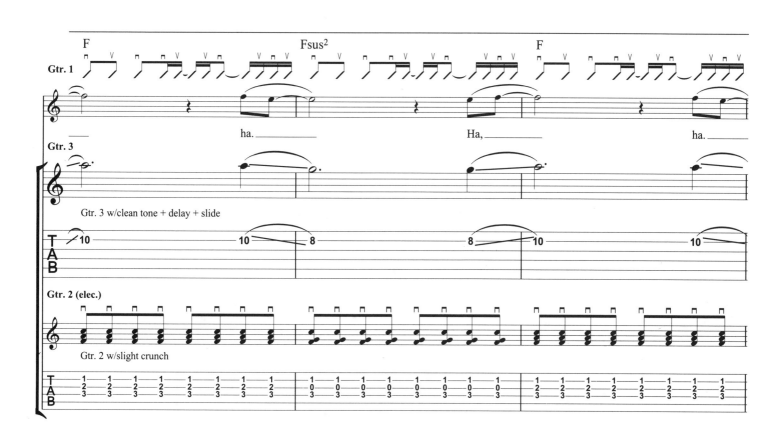

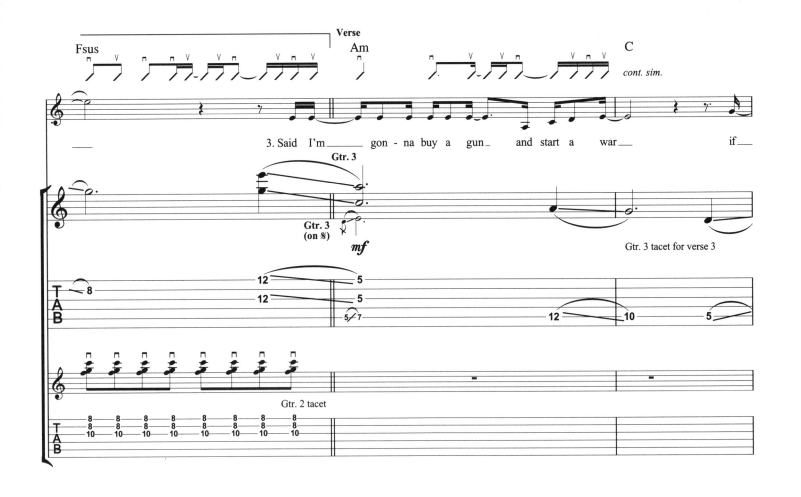

3. Said I'm___ gon - na buy a gun___ and start a war___ if___

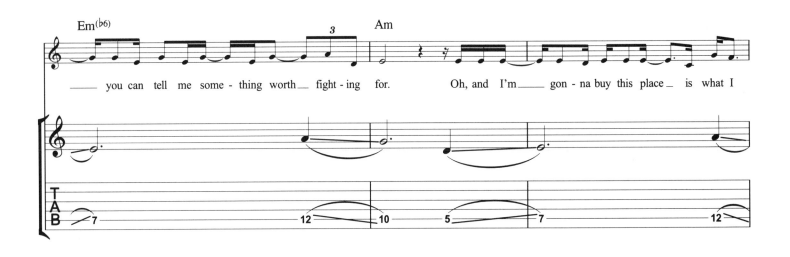

___ you can tell me some - thing worth___ fight - ing for. Oh, and I'm___ gon - na buy this place___ is what I

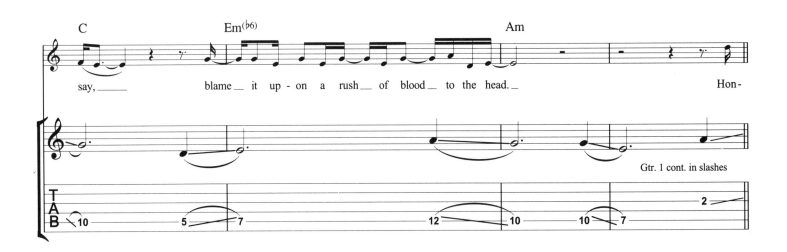

say,___ blame___ it up - on a rush___ of blood___ to the head.___ Hon -

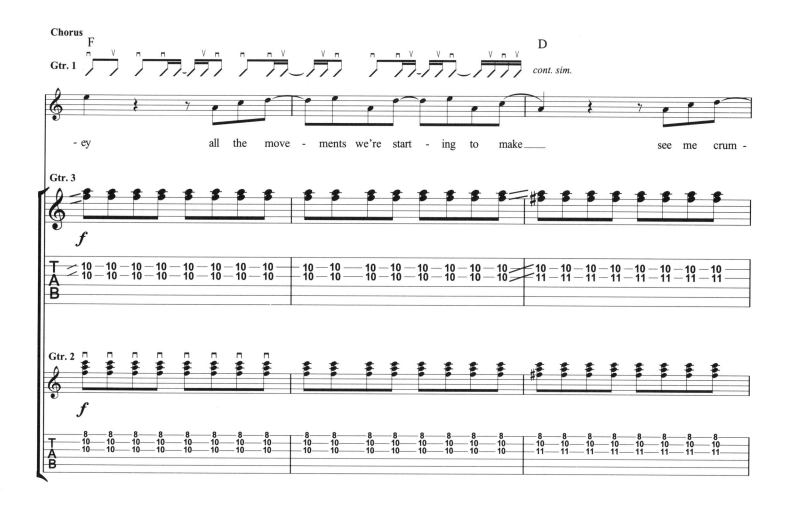

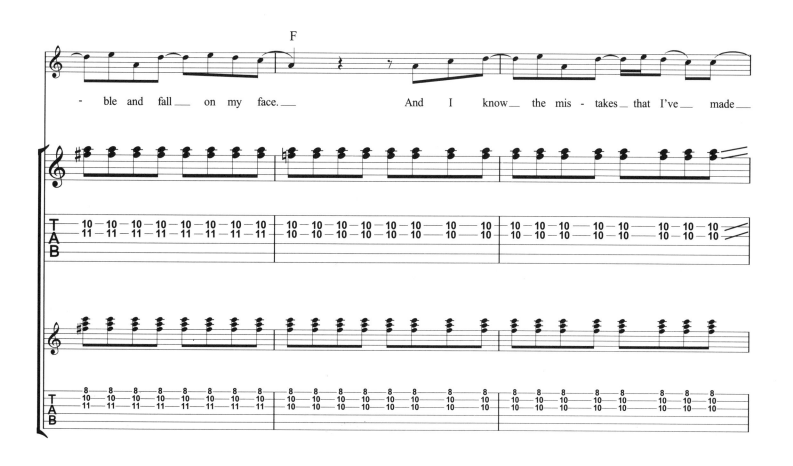

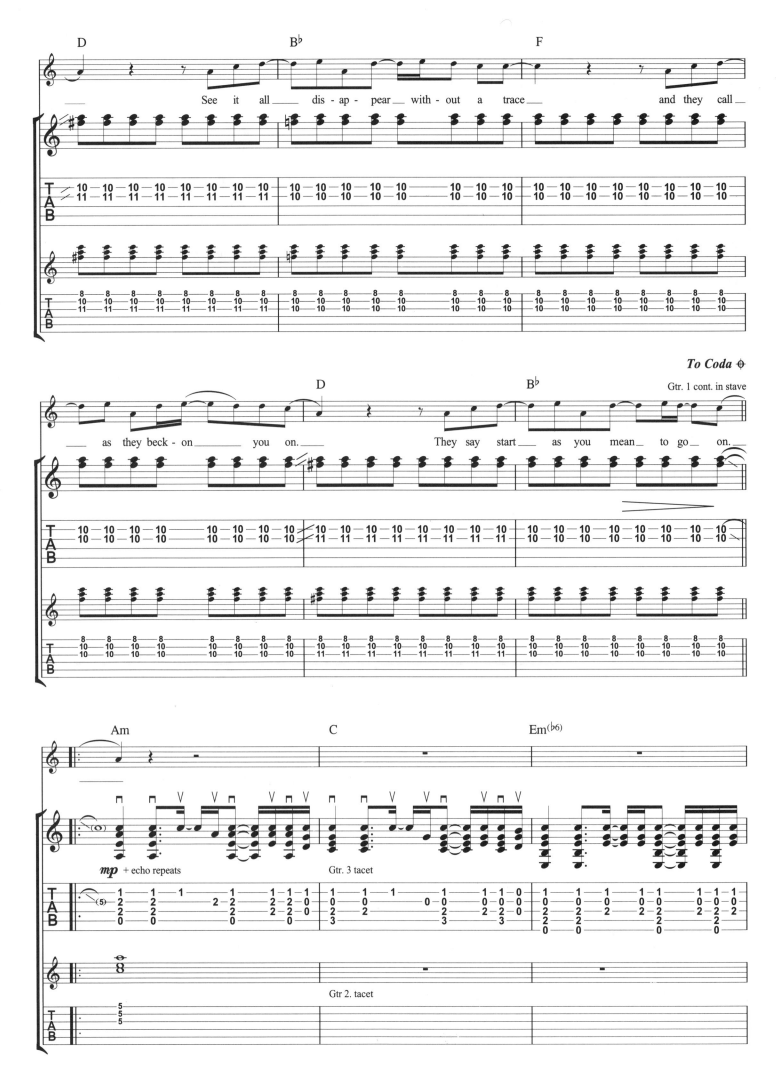

See it all ___ dis - ap - pear ___ with - out a trace ___ and they call ___

as they beck - on ___ you on. ___ They say start ___ as you mean ___ to go ___ on. ___

To Coda ⊕

Gtr. 1 cont. in stave

Gtr. 3 tacet

mp + echo repeats

Gtr 2. tacet

72

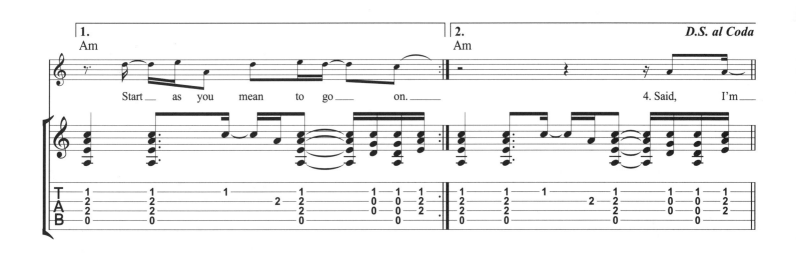

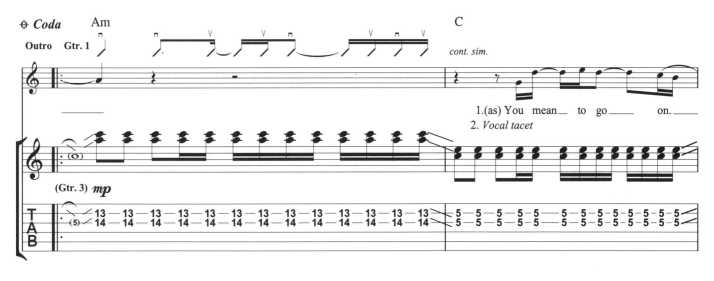

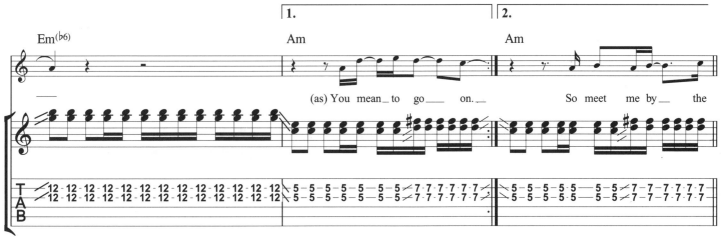

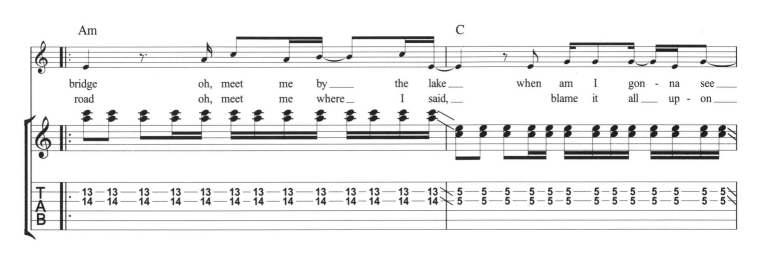

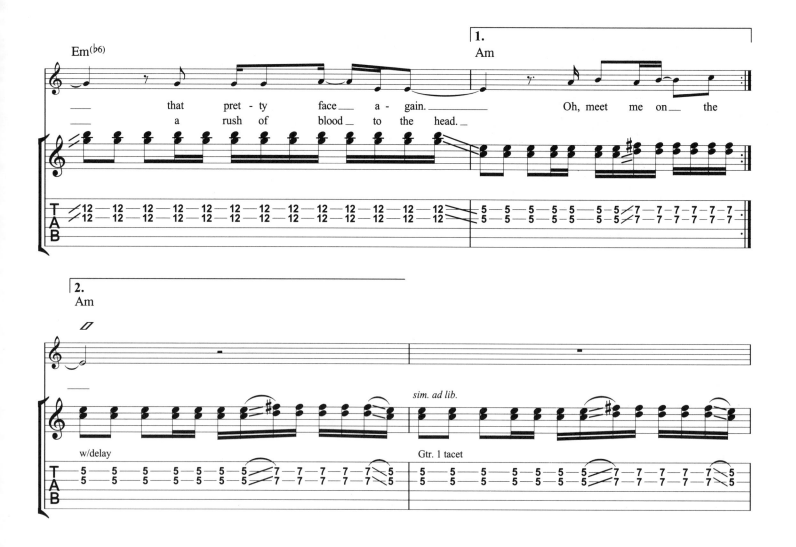

that pret-ty face___ a-gain._____ Oh, meet me on___ the

a rush of blood___ to the head.___

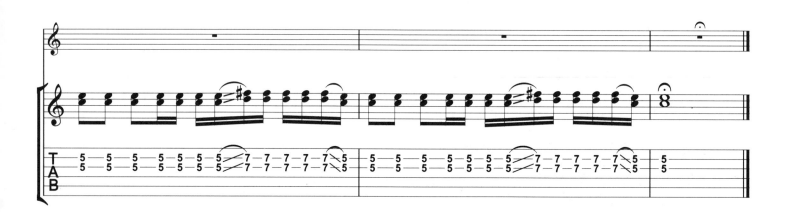

Verse 4 (𝄋):
Said I'm gonna buy this place and see it go
And stand here beside me baby, watch the orange glow
Some'll laugh and some just sit and cry
But you just sit down then you wonder why.

Verse 5:
So I'm gonna buy a gun *etc.*

Amsterdam

Words & Music by Guy Berryman, Jon Buckland, Will Champion & Chris Martin

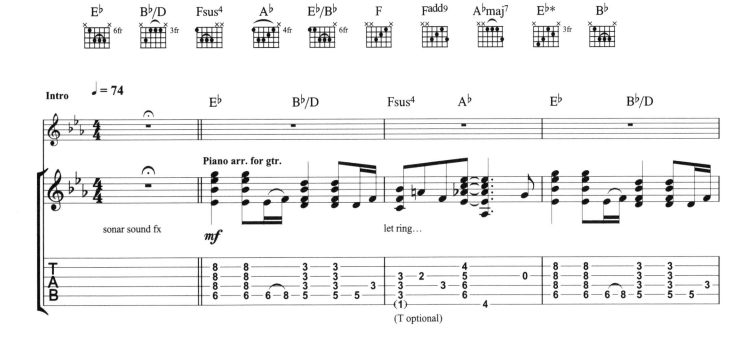

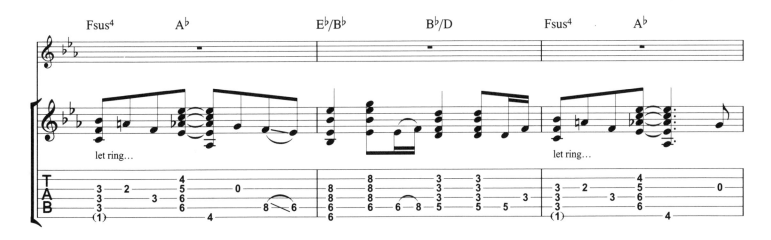

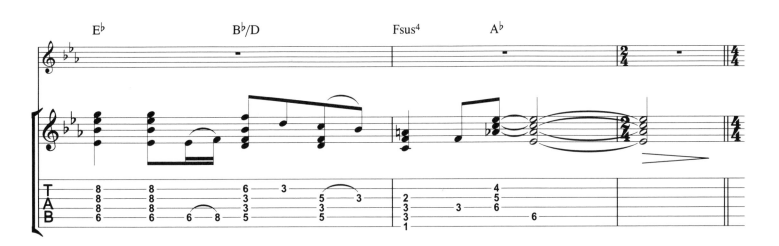

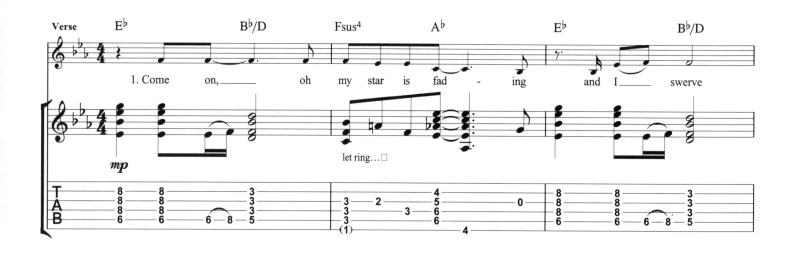

Verse

1. Come on, _____ oh my star is fad - ing and I _____ swerve

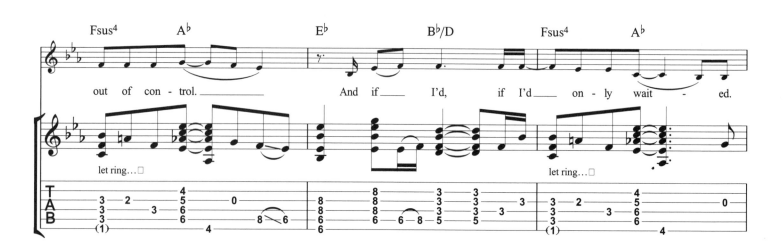

out of con - trol. _____ And if _____ I'd, if I'd _____ on - ly wait - ed.

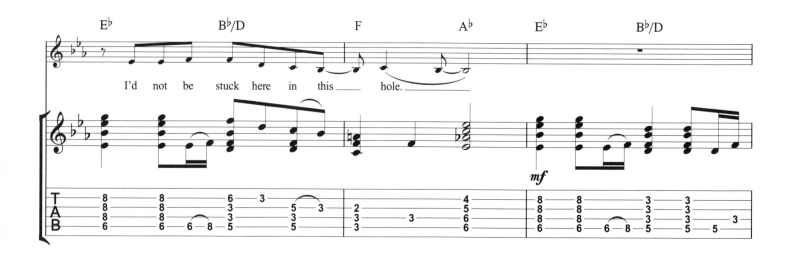

I'd not be stuck here in this _____ hole. _____

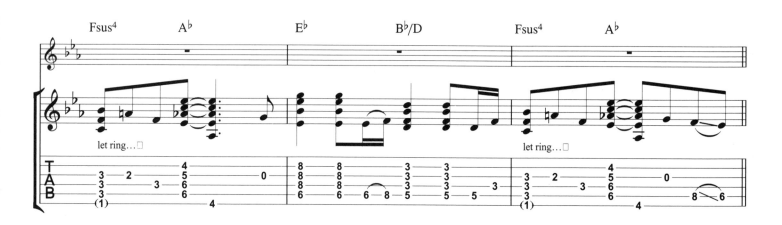

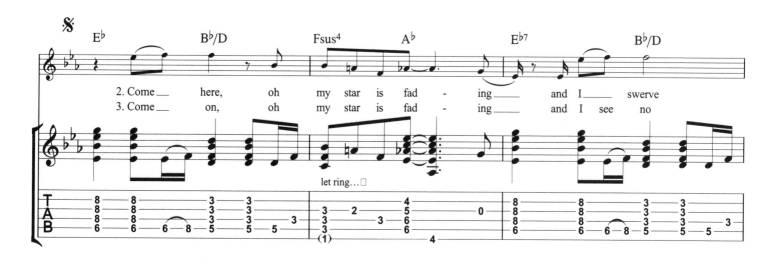

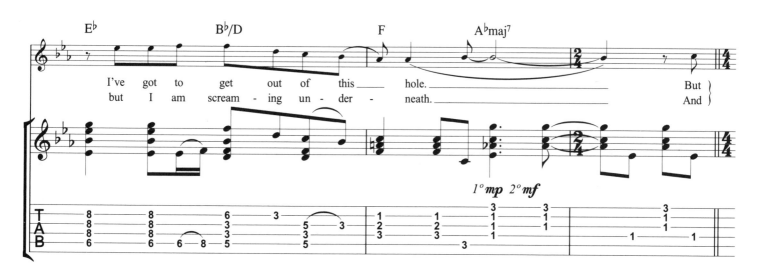

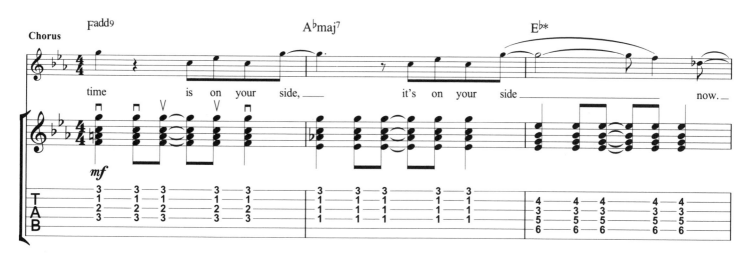

77

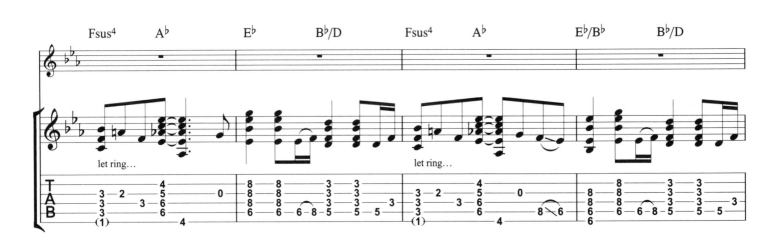

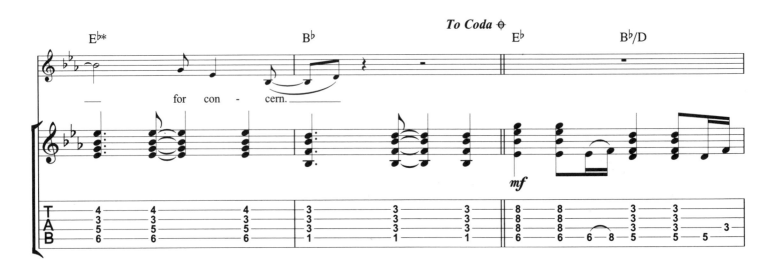

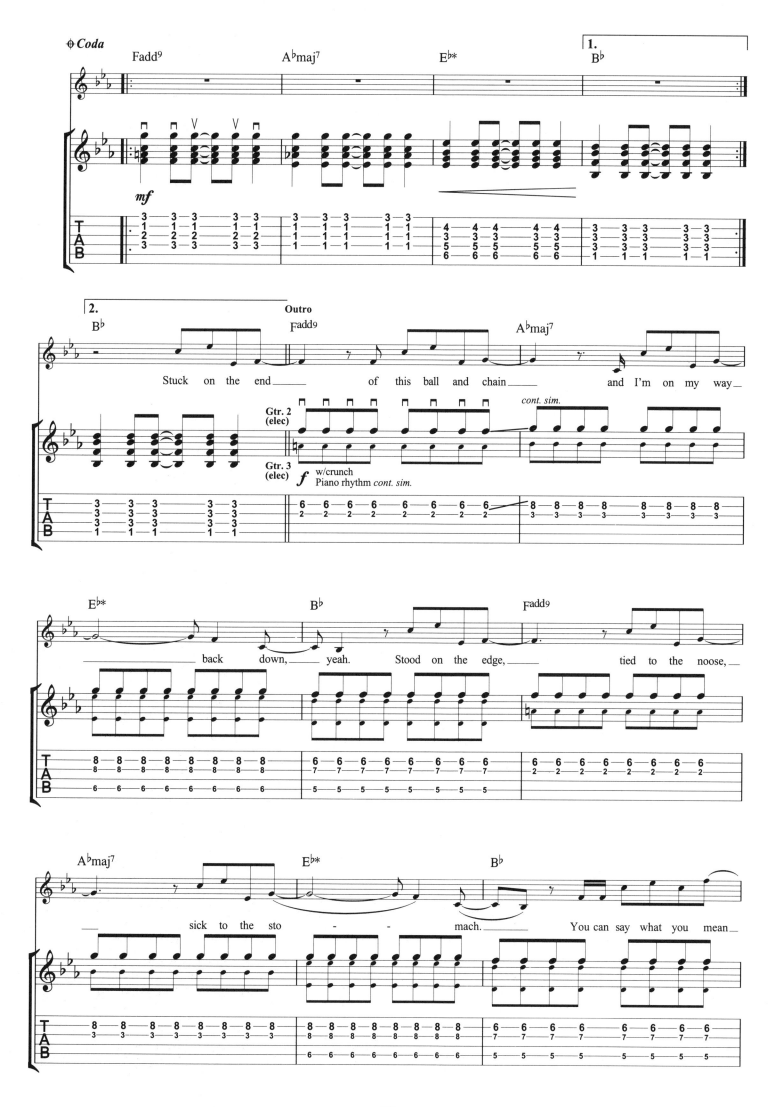

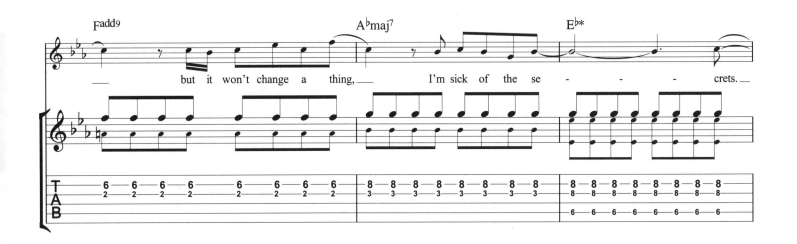

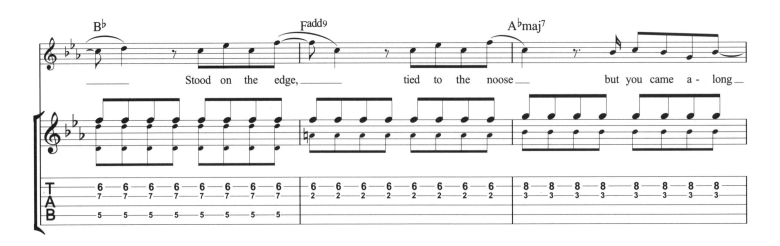

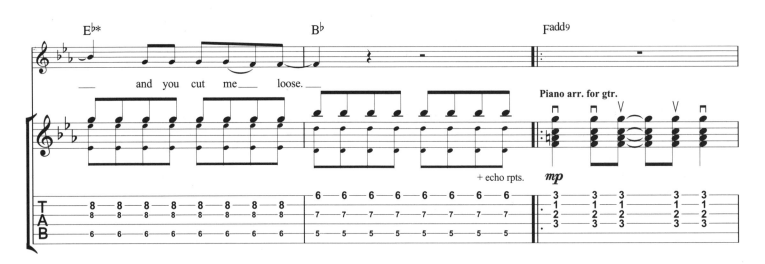

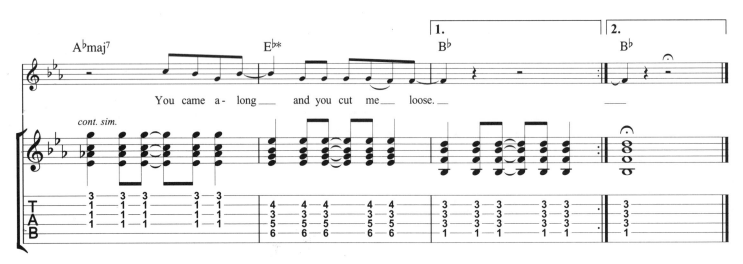